VEGETARIAN sandwiches

Fresh Fillings for
Slices, Pockets, Wraps, and Rolls

VEGETARIAN sandwiches

BY Paulette Mitchell

PHOTOGRAPHS BY Ondine Vierra

CHRONICLE BOOKS
SAN FRANCISCO

dedication
To my dad, who taught me that the best sandwiches are those shared with someone you love.

acknowledgments
Thank you to my editor, Bill LeBlond, a nonvegetarian who ordered the memorable vegetarian sandwich that inspired this book, and my appreciation for his enthusiasm and help in making this project a reality. Thank you also to my valued agent, Jane Dystel, who is always there with advice and support.

The production of this book is the result of the collaboration of many talented individuals at Chronicle. Thank you to Stephanie Rosenbaum and Jan Hughes, who skillfully and efficiently saw the book through editorial; Julia Flagg for her creative design; and Ondine Vierra for the vibrant photographs.

Library of Congress Cataloging-in-Publication Data:
Mitchell, Paulette.
Vegetarian sandwiches: fresh fillings for
slices, pockets, wraps, and rolls /
by Paulette Mitchell: photographs by Ondine Vierra.
p. cm.
ISBN 0-8118-2501-9 (pb.)
1. Sandwiches. 2. Vegetarian Cookery. I. Title
TX818.M58 2000
641.8'4—dc21
99-40536
CIP

Printed in Hong Kong

Prop styling by Carol Hacker
Food styling by Basil Friedman
Designed by Julia Flagg

Distributed in Canada by Raincoast Books
8680 Cambie Street
Vancouver, British Columbia V6P 6M9

1 2 3 4 5 6 7 8 9 10

Chronicle Books
85 Second Street
San Francisco, California 94105

www.chroniclebooks.com

contents

WHEN I THINK OF SANDWICHES, I RECALL CHILDHOOD SUNDAYS, the years before my Catholic mom learned to drive and my Jewish father dropped us at church, then continued on to Myer's Delicatessen. Sometimes, I'd convince Dad to let me tag along, promising not to interrupt while he and his best friend, Myer, discussed the week's events. I'd prove my worth by helping Dad choose the makings for our after-church lunch sandwich buffet. It was in Myer's Deli that I ventured beyond my safe realm of peanut butter and jelly on squishy white bread. Myer, dressed in his clean white butcher's coat, smiled from behind his glass-fronted deli case, offering tastes from the "old world," samples of imported Swiss and sharp English Cheddar. I'd nibble, savoring the distinct flavors of hearty Jewish rye and crusty onion rolls, then bite into a giant dill pickle that dribbled juice down my chin.

As a teenager, I improved my high-school lunch-table status by sharing quarters of imported cheese sandwiches and zesty bites of marinated vegetables, all from the family deli. Who could refuse these vibrant flavors, especially when faced with a mundane sandwich of tasteless processed cheese or dry bologna? Today, as the mother of a teenage son, I've found that these beloved deli standards make a nutritious lunch and a healthful alternative to typical American fast food on nights we rush to lessons or games. I'm often amazed at the assortment of vegetables my son and his friends will try as long as they are concealed in a "sub." And we've made a family tradition of eating grilled cheese sandwiches and tomato soup on rainy days: comfort.

Happily, sandwiches have kept up with the times, entering up-scale circles with trendy ingredients, while retaining their down-home appeal. In a tony New York restaurant in Soho, I recently lunched on a grilled portobello mushroom on a crusty whole-grain sesame bun, while my sophisticated friend tackled a tower of roasted eggplant and bright arugula slathered with aioli on sun-dried tomato bread.

The Brits lay claim to the very first sandwich, created as a royal meal for busy Sir John Montague. This eighteenth-century Englishman, a.k.a. the Fourth Earl of Sandwich, was a skilled gambler. Reluctant to miss even a few minutes away from his game, he instructed his servant to place meat between two slices of bread so that he could eat with one hand and take bites between bets. British sandwiches have climbed from the gaming to the tea table as crustless two-bite delicacies of watercress-garnished cucumber slices to nibble between sips of Earl Grey.

Just about every country owns a version of this simple, portable meal. Take the corner stands in Israel that sell felafel-stuffed pitas laced with a tangy mint sauce, or the Greek gyros drizzled with a mixture of tart yogurt and cucumber. And puns aside, the Italians hold the whole sandwich world in their capable, garden-inspired hands.

On a recent trip through Lazio, Tuscany, and the Veneto, each day spurred a search for sandwiches to sustain us through our museum and sightseeing jaunts. I joined the midday crowds of locals in Rome, where it has become fashion to stand at the counter of tiny espresso bars to lunch on bruschetta. The breads were tooth-tugging dense and satisfying, laying a fine foundation for field greens and roasted vegetables anointed with peppery olive oil and aged balsamic vinegar. On several balmy fall evenings in Florence, we people-watched at elegant outdoor cafés in the Piazza della Signoria, while we sipped aperitifs and snacked on crostini—less-filling, more delicate versions of bruschetta, topped with sun-warmed tomatoes, fresh basil, meaty olives, and a sprinkling of freshly grated Parmigiano-Reggiano. In Venice, we sat in St. Mark's Square, lunching on tramezzini— thin, elegant sandwiches made with crustless fresh white bread spread with garlic mayonnaise and filled with spicy arugula, hard-cooked egg, cucumber, and radish.

And sandwiches have been elevated to high art in America. Remember the Dagwood sandwich, that toppling wonder precariously balanced between two spongy slices of white? A sandwich is the serendipitous combination of creativity and great ingredients. Most of all, making and eating sandwiches is fun. Thanks to the wide availability of sensational ready-to-use spreads, condiments, interesting cheeses, and exotic components, great sandwiches can be made using a wide variety of freshly baked breads. Artisan bread shops are springing up everywhere, providing handmade loaves from rustic traditions, and supermarket bakers are refining their fresh-baked selections to keep up. A plethora of bagel shops dot city streets and shopping mall corridors, offering unusual bagels and new-fangled spreads. Bread, once a bland "carrier," has become a star ingredient to sandwich success.

These days, meals are themselves often sandwiched between competing activities. A homemade two-fisted hoagie can nourish the frazzled parent and starving soccer player, the jet-lagged executive, and the sleepy grad student. Cooking, if any, is minimal, so more time and thought can be spent in sandwich creation. Unfettered by any specific tradition, all sandwiches are open to interpretation. Within these pages you will find any number of sandwich ideas that fuse ethnic ingredients in nontraditional ways. I hope you'll feel free to mix and match the sandwich components to suit your taste.

The only rule is to make your sandwiches using top-quality ingredients: the best bread you can buy, seasonal produce, fresh herbs, imported cheeses, spreads with personality, and tasty condiments. Your sandwiches will only be as good as the ingredients you choose. Beyond that, there are no rules, except to ignore the rules, and be sure to eat with your hands.

the sandwich plan NOT BY BREAD ALONE

The combinations of breads, spreads or sauces, and fillings or toppings in the sandwiches in this book were devised to complement each other in texture and flavor, pairing spicy with mild, crunchy with creamy and smooth. Most often, one component is the star, and the others the supporting players. Garnishes are suggested to add zest or color. Don't hesitate to mix and match the spreads and fillings to suit your taste. Served on toast, most spreads will make terrific appetizers and accompaniments to soups and salads. I've included tips to guide you in selecting, storing, and preparing the best ingredients (see chart on page 11 for page references). And the advance preparation information will benefit you in planning ahead; some sandwiches will hold for several hours or even overnight when wrapped in plastic and refrigerated.

The recipes also include recommendations for breads, all widely available, or you may use others, as you prefer. Bread shops offer unsliced loaves that you can have custom sliced. An unsliced loaf will keep fresh longer and can be sliced as needed. For the cleanest cuts, use a serrated bread knife in a sawing motion. Some specialized bread knives are designed to be adjusted for cutting uniform thin or thick slices.

The ideal sandwich bread is fresh but not excessively doughy; it provides a textural balance for fillings, standing up to the weight of moist ingredients without dissolving into mush. Whole-grain breads are nutritionally superior to white breads and have more flavor and texture. Rye breads are more assertive and heavier; some are lightened with white flour. Breads flavored with ingredients such as sun-dried tomatoes, herbs, spices, cheese, olives, nuts, and dried fruits may enhance a sandwich if compatible with its filling. Breads with especially intense flavors usually are best served plain with soup, salad, or pasta. More neutral-tasting slices make a perfect canvas for brightly flavored sandwiches. You may also vary the bread's texture, making it crisp and sturdy by toasting it in the oven, or softer and moister by heating it in the microwave. It all depends on the filling.

Must all sandwiches "sandwich"? Not focaccia, the round or square Italian flat bread baked plain or topped with cheese or herbs. Bruschetta, another Italian specialty, is garlicky-olive oil toasts topped with savory specialties. Some "sandwiches" are wraps, made from rolled tortillas and flat breads, or stuffed pita bread pockets.

Served for a casual supper or brown bag lunch, as a quick meal for kids on the go, sliced into finger-sized snacks for afternoon tea or as simple hors d'oeuvres, or accompanying soup or salad, sandwiches may be designed to suit any occasion. Rather than assembling individual sandwiches for a crowd, prepare large whole-meal sandwiches in advance using focaccia or baguettes; to serve, just slice them into wedges or slices.

The recipes in this book are versatile. They double or halve easily. Adjust the quantities to use more of the ingredients you like best, or substitute others you have on hand. Use nonfat, low-fat, or regular dairy products;

regular or low-sodium soy sauce; homemade mustard and mayonnaise; or products off the supermarket shelf—whatever suits you best.

Many of the components for the sandwiches in this book can be purchased ready-made in the store, but when quality is of the utmost importance, homemade tastes best. The straightforward and simple recipes have been devised with an eye on the clock, and may be prepared in advance.

I've included a chapter of sandwich accompaniments to help in planning a meal. Besides, a sandwich often looks more appealing on the plate when there is another meal component on the side.

In these pages you'll find classic vegetarian standbys, such as Middle Eastern Pita Pockets stuffed with Tabbouleh and Hummus (page 100), and Tempeh Reubens (page 84), as well as ethnic delights, such as East Indian Tea Sandwiches (page 55) and Italian bruschetta (page 33), crostini (page 33), and tramezzini (page 46). I've included my favorite contemporary creations, such as Grilled Portobello Mushroom Sandwiches with Sun-Dried Tomato and Goat Cheese Spread (page 73), and Sweet Potato and Avocado Sandwiches with Tahini–Poppy Seed Spread (page 58). There are even sweet sandwich concoctions for brunch, snacks, or dessert. Enjoy these any time: served with style to guests at a candlelit table or by the light of your own refrigerator at midnight.

sandwich BASICS

Interesting homemade sauces and spreads make simple salads and sandwiches extraordinary. A thin coat of a spread, such as Mayonnaise (page 21), Honey Mustard (page 20), or Black Olive and Caper Spread (page 19), not only helps keep the bread from becoming soggy but also adds flavor. These basics may be prepared in advance and stored several days in the refrigerator; some can be frozen for longer storage.

These recipes are a gracenote in the busy cook's kitchen, for their uses abound. You'll find them as ingredients in recipes throughout the book. And, I often toss the Basil Pesto (page 16) with pasta, top a baked potato with Herb Butter (page 22), serve the Marinated Goat Cheese (page 23) atop a salad, and use Guacamole (page 18) alone as an appetizer dip for tortilla chips. Honey Mustard (page 20); Apricot, Pear, and Apple Chutney (page 28); and Roasted Red Bell Pepper Sauce (page 27) make thoughtful gifts from your kitchen.

TIPS

Here are the definitions for culinary terms frequently used in these recipes:

CHOP: To cut food into uniform shapes of small size, usually $\frac{1}{2}$ inch to 1 inch

DICE: To cut food into small cubes or squares, usually $\frac{1}{8}$ inch to $\frac{1}{4}$ inch

JULIENNE: To cut foods into matchstick strips, about $\frac{1}{8}$-inch wide

MINCE: To cut pieces of food into very small bits, no larger than $\frac{1}{8}$ inch; often used for fresh herbs

SHRED: To cut food into narrow strips; use a knife, grater, or a food processor fitted with a shredding disk.

Sun-Dried Tomato Pesto

MAKES ¹/₂ CUP

THIS PESTO IS INTENSELY FLAVORED. USE IT AS IS FOR A SANDWICH SPREAD IN
WARM VEGGIE HOAGIES (PAGE 83). SPREAD IT ON SLICED BAGELS AND BROIL, OR COMBINE IT
IN EQUAL AMOUNTS WITH MAYONNAISE, FRESH WHITE GOAT CHEESE, OR PLAIN YOGURT FOR
USE IN YOUR OTHER SANDWICH CREATIONS.

¹/₄ cup oil-packed minced sun-dried tomatoes;
drain and reserve oil (see Tips)

1 tablespoon reserved oil from sun-dried tomatoes

1 tablespoon concentrated tomato paste (see Tips)

1 tablespoon fresh lemon juice

2 cloves garlic, minced, or
1 teaspoon prepared minced garlic

¹/₄ teaspoon freshly ground pepper, or to taste

¹/₄ teaspoon red pepper flakes, or to taste (see Tips)

Salt to taste

1 tablespoon minced fresh flat-leaf parsley

Process all the ingredients, except the parsley, in a food processor until smooth. Stir in the parsley. Taste and adjust the seasoning.

ADVANCE PREPARATION
*This pesto will keep for up to 1 week
in a tightly covered container in the refrigerator.
For longer storage, freeze it in a small container
for up to 2 months.*

TIPS

Because they are flavorful and easy to use, I prefer to purchase jars of sun-dried tomatoes that have been rehydrated and packed in olive oil; they must be refrigerated after opening. Drain off the excess oil before using. (The oil can be reserved, refrigerated, and used in recipes calling for olive oil, especially those with tomatoes as an ingredient.) Dried tomatoes that are not marinated in oil will keep in an airtight container for several months; they must be rehydrated before using in many recipes. Cover them with boiling water and soak for about 10 to 15 minutes or until moist, then drain off the water. Use the tomatoes immediately or marinate them in olive oil (be sure to refrigerate) for later use.

Concentrated tomato paste is available in tubes, ideal for recipes calling for less than a 6-ounce can. Refrigerate the tube after opening.

Red pepper flakes, also called crushed red pepper, are the seeds and flakes of fiery hot peppers; a small amount goes a long way! Refrigerate in a tightly covered container to preserve the color and flavor.

Basil Pesto

MAKES 1/3 CUP

MAKING THIS PESTO HAS BECOME A SEPTEMBER TRADITION FOR ME. AT THE END OF THE GROWING SEASON, BEFORE THE FIRST FROST, I PINCH OFF THE LEAVES REMAINING ON MY BASIL PLANTS AND PREPARE THE AROMATIC BLEND. IT'S A TREAT TO PULL IT FROM THE FREEZER TO TOSS WITH PASTA OR TO USE AS A TASTY SANDWICH SPREAD, ALONE OR MIXED WITH MAYONNAISE.

TIP

To store fresh herbs, wrap the stem ends in a moist paper towel and refrigerate in a sealed plastic bag. Or, place the bunch, stems down, in a glass of water and cover with a plastic bag, securing the bag to the glass with a rubber band; change the water every 2 days. With proper storage, fresh herbs will last for about 1 week, but for the best flavor, use them within a few days. Just before using, wash fresh herbs in cool water, then dry them with paper towels or in a salad spinner.

1 cup loosely packed fresh basil leaves (see Tip)

1/4 cup pine nuts

2 tablespoons extra-virgin olive oil

2 cloves garlic, minced, or
1 teaspoon prepared minced garlic

1/4 teaspoon freshly ground pepper

Salt to taste

Process all the ingredients in a food processor until the mixture is a coarse purée. Using a rubber spatula, scrape down the sides as needed.

VARIATION

Substitute chopped pecans for the pine nuts.

ADVANCE PREPARATION
This pesto will keep for up to 1 week in a covered container in the refrigerator; pour a thin film of olive oil on top of the pesto to prevent discoloration. For longer storage, spoon the mixture, in 2-tablespoon quantities, into foil-lined custard cups or muffin tins; cover tightly with foil and freeze. Once frozen, remove the foil-wrapped packets and store in a freezer bag for up to 2 months. To use, thaw in the refrigerator overnight, or remove from the foil and thaw quickly in the microwave.

Hummus

MAKES 1¼ CUPS

FOR AN OPEN-FACED SANDWICH APPETIZER, SPREAD HUMMUS ON SMALL SQUARES OF WHITE BREAD AND TOP WITH THIN CUCUMBER SLICES AND BITS OF CHERRY TOMATOES. THIS AROMATIC SPREAD IS ALSO AN INGREDIENT IN MIDDLE EASTERN PITA POCKETS (PAGE 100). USE LEFTOVER HUMMUS AS A DIP FOR FRESH VEGETABLES OR AS A SPREAD FOR CRACKERS. THE FLAVOR ACTUALLY IMPROVES IF HUMMUS IS MADE IN ADVANCE, SO PLAN AHEAD A DAY OR TWO.

----

1 tablespoon canola oil

¼ cup minced red onion

2 cloves garlic, minced, or
1 teaspoon prepared minced garlic

¼ cup minced fresh flat-leaf parsley (see Tips)

1 tablespoon minced fresh basil, or
½ teaspoon dried basil

1 teaspoon minced fresh oregano, or
½ teaspoon dried oregano

¼ teaspoon ground coriander

¼ teaspoon freshly ground pepper, or to taste

⅛ teaspoon ground cumin, or to taste

One 15-ounce can garbanzo beans,
drained and rinsed (see Tips)

3 tablespoons fresh lemon juice

2 tablespoons toasted sesame seeds (see Tip, page 44)

Salt to taste

ADVANCE PREPARATION
Hummus will keep for up to 5 days in a covered container in the refrigerator. Bring to room temperature before serving.

Heat the oil in a small skillet over medium-high heat. Add the onion and garlic; cook, stirring occasionally, until aromatic and tender, about 3 minutes. Remove from the heat; stir in the parsley, basil, oregano, coriander, pepper, and cumin.

Process the garbanzo beans and lemon juice in a food processor until the mixture is smooth. Add the bean mixture, sesame seeds, and salt to the skillet; stir until evenly combined. Taste and adjust the seasoning. Let cool.

VARIATION

WHITE BEAN HUMMUS: Substitute olive oil for the canola oil and one 15-ounce can white beans for the garbanzos. Because white beans are moister, reduce the lemon juice to 2 tablespoons.

TIPS

Flat-leaf parsley, also called Italian parsley, has a more pungent flavor and is preferable to the more common curly-leaf parsley. Wash fresh parsley and shake off the excess moisture, then wrap the parsley in damp paper towels and store it in a plastic bag in the refrigerator for up to 1 week. Avoid using dried parsley, which has little of the distinctive parsley flavor.

To mince parsley very finely, be sure to dry it well with a paper towel or dish towel after cleaning it under cool running water. Wet or damp parsley will stick together in clumps as you mince it with a knife or in a food processor.

Garbanzo beans are sometimes called chickpeas, ceci beans, or Spanish beans. They are nut-like in flavor and similar to hazelnuts in shape and size. Cooking dried garbanzo beans from scratch requires 8 hours of soaking and 3 hours of cooking; canned garbanzo beans are a good alternative.

Guacamole

MAKES ABOUT 2/3 CUP

USE THIS AS A CREAMY SPREAD IN MEXICAN BLACK BEAN PITAS (PAGE 104) AND ON THE BUNS FOR SAVORY NUT PATTIES ON SESAME BUNS (PAGE 89), OR ADD IT ALONG WITH SLICED TOMATOES AND LETTUCE TO PERK UP AN ORDINARY CHEESE SANDWICH. ADJUST THE AMOUNT OF HOT PEPPER SAUCE TO MAKE THE SPREAD MILD OR ZESTY.

The two most common varieties of avocados are the Fuerte, which has a smooth green skin, and the pebbly textured, almost black, rich-flavored Haas, which I prefer. Select fruits that are unblemished and heavy for their size. Most avocados require a few days of ripening after purchasing; place them in a pierced paper bag at room temperature for a day or two to speed up the process. The avocados will yield to a gentle pressure when they are ripe and ready to use. Store ripe avocados in the refrigerator for up to 5 days. Once cut and exposed to the air, avocado flesh discolors rapidly; to minimize this, coat the cut surfaces with lime or lemon juice, and add these juices to recipes containing avocado.

1 ripe avocado, quartered and peeled (see Tip)

1 tablespoon fresh lime or lemon juice

1 tablespoon coarsely chopped onion

2 teaspoons plain yogurt

2 cloves garlic, minced, or 1 teaspoon prepared minced garlic

1/8 teaspoon hot pepper sauce, or to taste

1/8 teaspoon freshly ground pepper, or to taste

Salt to taste

Process all the ingredients in a food processor until the mixture is smooth and creamy. Taste and adjust the seasoning.

Refrigerate in a covered container for at least 1 hour before serving.

ADVANCE PREPARATION
This spread will keep for up to 2 days in a covered container in the refrigerator.

Black Olive and Caper Spread

MAKES 3/4 CUP

BASED ON THE CLASSIC FRENCH TAPENADE OF OLIVES, CAPERS, AND ANCHOVIES OR TUNA, THIS VEGETARIAN SPREAD MAKES A TASTY AND SLIGHTLY SALTY SANDWICH COMPONENT. PREPARE IT FOR OPEN-FACED CRISPY TORTILLA SANDWICHES (PAGE 61); USE THE EXTRA AS A SPREAD FOR BRUSCHETTA OR CROSTINI (PAGE 33).

One 4 1/2-ounce can chopped ripe olives, drained

1 tablespoon extra-virgin olive oil

1 tablespoon fresh lemon juice

2 teaspoons capers, drained and rinsed (see Tip)

2 cloves garlic, minced, or
1 teaspoon prepared minced garlic

Dash of freshly ground pepper, or to taste

1 tablespoon minced fresh flat-leaf parsley

Process all the ingredients, except the parsley, in a food processor until the mixture is a coarse purée. Using a rubber spatula, scrape down the sides as needed. Stir in the parsley. Taste and adjust the seasoning.

ADVANCE PREPARATION
This spread will keep for up to 3 days in a covered container in the refrigerator.

TIP
Capers are the unopened flower buds of a shrub native to the Mediterranean and parts of Asia. After drying in the sun, the buds are pickled in a vinegar brine. Capers come in several sizes; the largest have the strongest flavor. The smallest, called "nonpareil," are more subtle in taste, the most tender, and the most expensive. Capers should be rinsed before using to remove excess salt. Once the jar is opened, store capers in the refrigerator for up to 3 months.

Honey Mustard

MAKES ³/4 CUP

A STAPLE IN MY REFRIGERATOR, THIS ZESTY MUSTARD IS A CUT ABOVE BALLPARK MUSTARD.
IT ALSO HAS BECOME A HOLIDAY TRADITION, AS I MULTIPLY THE RECIPE AND SHARE JARS WITH
THE SANDWICH-LOVERS ON MY CHRISTMAS LIST.

¹/2 cup dry mustard

¹/2 cup white rice vinegar

1 egg

¹/3 cup honey

ADVANCE PREPARATION
This mustard will keep for up to 3 months in a tightly closed container in the refrigerator.

Combine the mustard and vinegar in a small bowl; whisk to remove any lumps. Cover and let stand at room temperature for at least 4 hours or overnight.

Pour the mustard mixture into a blender; add the egg and honey. Blend until smooth.

In a double boiler over simmering water (see Tips), cook the mustard mixture, whisking constantly, until the mixture thickens to a pudding consistency, about 5 minutes. Remove the top pan from the double boiler and let the mustard cool for about 5 minutes, stirring occasionally. Pour the mustard into a sterilized glass jar (see Tips); cover and refrigerate.

VARIATION
Use 1 pasteurized egg or ¹/4 cup cholesterol-free egg substitute if you are concerned about food safety.

Mayonnaise

MAKES 1 CUP

FOR SUCCESS IN MAKING HOMEMADE MAYONNAISE IN YOUR BLENDER,
BEGIN WITH ALL THE INGREDIENTS AT ROOM TEMPERATURE.

-----

1 egg

2 tablespoons white wine vinegar or white rice vinegar (see Tips)

2 teaspoons honey

⅛ teaspoon dry mustard (see Tips)

⅛ teaspoon ground white pepper, or to taste

Salt to taste

¾ cup canola oil

ADVANCE PREPARATION
This mayonnaise will keep for up to 1 week in a tightly closed container in the refrigerator.

Blend all the ingredients, except the oil, in a blender until smooth. With the machine running, add the oil very slowly in a steady, thin stream, until the mixture is well combined and thickened. (Homemade mayonnaise will not be as thick as purchased mayonnaise.) Taste and adjust the seasoning. Transfer the mayonnaise to a glass container with a tight-fitting lid.

VARIATIONS
Substitute extra-virgin olive oil for the canola oil if an olive oil flavor is compatible with your sandwich ingredients.

Use 1 pasteurized egg or ¼ cup cholesterol-free egg substitute if you are concerned about using raw eggs in this uncooked mixture.

GARLIC MAYONNAISE: Add 4 cloves garlic, or 2 teaspoons prepared minced garlic, with the first group of ingredients.

BASIL MAYONNAISE: Stir ¼ cup Basil Pesto (page 16) into the completed mayonnaise (preferably made with extra-virgin olive oil); add an extra dash of salt and some freshly ground pepper.

HERB MAYONNAISE: Stir 1 to 2 tablespoons minced fresh herbs, such as flat-leaf parsley, watercress, basil, oregano, or tarragon, into the completed mayonnaise.

TIPS

White rice vinegar, made from fermented rice, has a low acidity and is milder and sweeter than ordinary white vinegar. It can be found in Asian markets and most supermarkets.

Dry mustard is finely ground mustard seeds. Store it in a dark, dry place for up to 6 months.

Yogurt Cheese

MAKES 1 CUP

WHEN PLAIN YOGURT IS STRAINED, THE LIQUID WHEY DRAINS OFF, LEAVING A THICK, TART CHEESE THAT MAKES A FINE ALTERNATIVE TO CREAM CHEESE, AND CAN ALSO BE USED IN PLACE OF MAYONNAISE.

One 16-ounce carton fresh plain yogurt, whole milk, low-fat, or nonfat (do not use yogurt with gelatin added); see Tips

ADVANCE PREPARATION
If you begin with fresh yogurt, the yogurt cheese will keep for up to 1 week in a tightly covered container in the refrigerator.

Set a strainer over a large bowl (make certain the strainer does not touch the bottom of the bowl). Line the strainer with 4 layers of cheesecloth, allowing about 4 inches to extend over the sides of the strainer.

Spoon the yogurt into the strainer. Gather the cheesecloth together; fold the ends over the yogurt. Or, line the strainer with a paper coffee filter. Cover the strainer and bowl with plastic wrap. Refrigerate for at least 8 hours or overnight. Transfer the yogurt cheese to a covered container; discard the cheesecloth and the liquid.

Herb Butter

MAKES 1/2 CUP

THIS IS A MUST ON ITALIAN TOASTED CHEESE SANDWICHES (PAGE 86); ALSO TRY IT ON STEAMED VEGETABLES OR USE IT TO DRESS UP BAKED POTATOES.

1/2 cup (1 stick) unsalted butter at room temperature

1 tablespoon freshly grated Parmesan cheese

1 clove garlic, minced, or 1/2 teaspoon prepared minced garlic

2 teaspoons minced fresh flat-leaf parsley

2 teaspoons snipped fresh chives (see Tips)

2 teaspoons snipped fresh dill, or 1/4 teaspoon dried dill (see Tips)

Dash of ground white pepper

Beat the butter in a small bowl with an electric mixer until it is light and fluffy. Use a rubber spatula to fold in the remaining ingredients.

VARIATION
Substitute other fresh herbs (up to 4 teaspoons), such as basil or thyme, for the chives and dill.

ADVANCE PREPARATION
This butter will keep for up to 1 week in a tightly closed glass container in the refrigerator.

TIPS

Check the expiration date when buying yogurt; if refrigerated, it will keep for up to 1 week beyond that date in a tightly closed container in the refrigerator. The watery layer in yogurt cartons is simply the whey rising to the top. Stir it back in; it has nothing to do with the age or quality of the yogurt.

Chives are a delicately flavored member of the onion family. If possible, buy potted chives or grow them in your garden. Use scissors to snip off what you need, cutting off whole blades rather than chopping the tops off all the blades. If you buy cut chives, wrap them in damp paper towels, seal in a plastic bag, and refrigerate for up to 1 week.

Dill is a sharply aromatic herb with a mild, lemony taste. When using fresh dill, cut the feathery dill tips with scissors. Dried dill is acceptable, but it is stronger than fresh, so use it in moderation.

Marinated Goat Cheese

MAKES ABOUT ¹/₂ CUP

HERE'S A WAY TO PROLONG THE LIFE OF FRESH WHITE GOAT CHEESE AND TO ADD FLAVOR
AT THE SAME TIME. KEEP MARINATED GOAT CHEESE ON HAND IN YOUR REFRIGERATOR TO USE
ON BRUSCHETTA OR CROSTINI (PAGE 33) OR AS A SPREAD FOR PORTOBELLO MUSHROOM
BURGERS (PAGE 90) OR MEDITERRANEAN ROLL-UPS WITH FETA-KALAMATA SPREAD (PAGE 107).

One 4- to 6-ounce log fresh white goat cheese (see Tip)

¹/₄ cup extra-virgin olive oil

**2 cloves garlic, minced, or
1 teaspoon prepared minced garlic**

1 teaspoon minced fresh rosemary

1 teaspoon minced fresh basil

¹/₂ teaspoon freshly ground pepper

Salt to taste

ADVANCE PREPARATION
*This cheese will keep in the refrigerator for up to
1 month, as long as it is covered by a thin
layer of olive oil.*

Cut the cheese log into 1-inch pieces; drop into an
8-ounce glass jar with a tight-fitting lid.

Stir the olive oil and all the remaining ingredients
together in a measuring cup; pour over the cheese.
Add more oil if necessary to cover the top of the
cheese. Cap the jar and shake to distribute the oil
and herbs.

Refrigerate for at least 2 hours before serving.
To serve, spoon out the cheese as needed, draining
off the excess oil.

TIP
Goat cheese (*chèvre* in French)
is made from goat's milk and
may be either fresh and white,
or coated with herbs, or aged to
varying degrees. Domestic goat
cheese is a fine substitute for
the more expensive imported
brands. Once opened, tightly
wrap fresh goat cheese in plastic and store it in the refrigerator for 1 to 2 weeks, or marinate
it in olive oil for longer storage.
(Do not confuse fresh white
goat cheese with feta cheese or
caprini, Italian goat cheese,
which is aged, less creamy, and
more acidic.)

Lemon Vinaigrette

MAKES ½ CUP

THIS VIBRANT DRESSING REQUIRES EXTRA-VIRGIN OLIVE OIL, FRESHLY SQUEEZED LEMON JUICE, AND FRESH OREGANO. TOSS WITH MIXED BABY GREENS (SEE TIPS) FOR A SIDE-DISH SALAD; USE TORN ROMAINE LETTUCE AND ADD TOMATO CHUNKS, CHOPPED CUCUMBER, CRUMBLED FETA CHEESE, AND SLICED OLIVES TO MAKE THE SALAD MORE SUBSTANTIAL. THIS DRESSING IS ALSO A COMPONENT OF POTATO SALAD WITH LEMON VINAIGRETTE (PAGE 117) AND A VARIATION FOR MARINATED OVEN-DRIED TOMATOES (PAGE 114).

(PAGE 117)

Mixed baby greens, also called mesclun, usually include arugula, frisée, mizuma, oak leaf lettuce, and radicchio. If refrigerated in a plastic bag, they will last for up to 5 days.

Freshly squeezed citrus juice is always the most flavorful. Avoid the chemical-laden and artificial-tasting reconstituted lemon and lime juices that come in bottles and plastic "lemons" and "limes."

To squeeze more juice from citrus fruits, first bring them to room temperature or microwave chilled fruit (pierce the fruit with a fork or knife first) for 30 seconds on high.

DOUBLING SALAD DRESS-INGS: Do not double the amount of herbs and spices; use just a little more than in the original recipe, then add more to taste. When dried herbs are used in a salad dressing, allow the dressing to stand for about half an hour before using, if possible, to soften the herbs and bring out their flavors. To adjust the seasonings in a dressing, taste by dipping a salad ingredient, such as a vegetable or lettuce leaf, into the dressing. Tasted from a spoon, most dressings seem very strong.

¼ cup extra-virgin olive oil

¼ cup fresh lemon juice (see Tips)

2 teaspoons minced fresh oregano, or ½ teaspoon dried oregano (see Tips)

2 cloves garlic, minced, or 1 teaspoon prepared minced garlic

½ teaspoon sugar

¼ teaspoon freshly ground pepper, or to taste

⅛ teaspoon salt, or to taste

Whisk all the ingredients together in a small bowl, making certain the sugar is dissolved. Taste and adjust the seasoning.

ADVANCE PREPARATION
This dressing will keep for up to 2 days in a tightly closed container in the refrigerator; shake or whisk before using.

Roasted Garlic

Roasting gives garlic a buttery texture and a rich, sweet flavor that is especially pleasing on warm sandwiches. It melts into the bread and adds its mellow flavor to every bite. Try roasted garlic on your Grilled Portobello Mushroom Sandwiches with Sun-Dried Tomato and Goat Cheese Spread (page 73), vegetarian burgers (pages 89 and 90), or on Bruschetta or Crostini (page 33), either solo or spread on the warm toasted bread before adding a topping. Roasted garlic also can be used as an ingredient in most recipes calling for garlic, including the spreads in this book.

----

1 or more whole garlic bulbs (see Tip)

Olive oil for brushing

ADVANCE PREPARATION
Roasted garlic bulbs will keep for up to 3 days wrapped in plastic wrap or in a tightly covered container in the refrigerator.

Preheat the oven to 400°F. Line a baking sheet or small pan with aluminum foil.

Gently remove the loose, excess papery skin from each garlic bulb. Trim off the top stem and $1/4$ to $1/2$ inch of the garlic head (exposing the cloves directly to the heat speeds up the roasting process), but leave the cloves intact. Brush the outer skin and top with about 1 teaspoon olive oil and place the bulb on the prepared pan. (You can roast as many at one time as you'd like.)

Bake the bulb (or bulbs) for about 20 to 25 minutes, or until the cloves feel very soft when pierced with the tip of a knife. Remove the bulb from the pan and let cool.

To use, separate the individual garlic cloves; slice the bottom from each and squeeze at the end to release the roasted garlic.

VARIATION
To roast garlic in the microwave: Place the prepared garlic bulb on a paper towel. Microwave on high for 1 minute; turn the bulb upside-down, then microwave for about 1 more minute.

TIP
Select garlic heads that are clean and firm to the touch. Store them in a cool, dark, well-ventilated place such as a garlic cellar (a ceramic pot with holes and a lid); or seal them in a plastic bag and refrigerate. Unbroken bulbs will keep for up to 2 months; once broken from the bulb, individual cloves will keep for up to 10 days. Sprouted garlic cloves are usable, but they are less flavorful.

Roasted Red Bell Peppers

Bell peppers are most often sold in the mature green stage, fully developed but not ripe. Red bell peppers are vine-ripened green peppers, and they are sweeter because of the longer ripening.

Choose bell peppers that are plump, firm, and crisp, with no wrinkling or soft spots. Store them for up to 1 week in plastic bags in the refrigerator.

ROASTED RED BELL PEPPERS PLAY A PART IN SEVERAL SAUCES AND SANDWICHES IN THIS BOOK. LET THEM INSPIRE YOUR OWN SANDWICHES, TOO. PREROASTED RED BELL PEPPERS ARE SOLD IN JARS, BUT I THINK ROASTING THEM YOURSELF IS BEST BECAUSE THEY ARE FRESHER TASTING. IT TAKES ONLY ABOUT HALF AN HOUR, AND THE PEPPERS WILL KEEP IN THE REFRIGERATOR FOR LATER USE.

---

1 or more red bell peppers (see Tips)

Olive oil for brushing

ADVANCE PREPARATION
Roasted bell peppers will keep for up to 2 days in a tightly closed container or plastic bag in the refrigerator. Drain well before using.

Preheat the broiler. Line a baking sheet with aluminum foil.

Remove the stem and cut each bell pepper in half lengthwise; discard the seeds, veins, and stem. Place the pepper halves, skin sides up, in a single layer on the prepared pan; flatten each with the palm of your hand. Lightly brush the skins with olive oil.

Broil for about 10 minutes, or until the pepper halves are fork-tender and the skins are blackened and blistered. Transfer the pepper halves to a self-sealing heavy-duty plastic bag and seal; set aside for about 10 to 15 minutes, or until cool. (The steam will loosen the skins.) Remove the pepper halves from the bag; peel and discard the skins.

VARIATIONS
Roast whole bell peppers on a grill over a hot charcoal fire or over the flame of a gas stove.

Marinate the roasted and peeled bell peppers in extra-virgin olive oil and season with salt and pepper or marinate them in Italian Marinade (page 114), Lemon Vinaigrette (page 24), Balsamic Marinade (page 115), or Walnut Vinaigrette (page 118).

Roasted Red Bell Pepper Sauce

MAKES ABOUT ³/4 CUP

THIS LUSCIOUS RED SAUCE IS A FULL-FLAVORED COMPONENT IN OPEN-FACED CRISPY TORTILLA SANDWICHES (PAGE 61). IT ALSO IS DELICIOUS DRIZZLED OVER STEAMED OR SAUTÉED VEGETABLES AS A SIDE DISH. IF TIME PERMITS, ROAST YOUR OWN PEPPER; FOR SPEEDIER PREPARATION, USE A JARRED PEPPER.

1 Roasted Red Bell Pepper (page 26) or jarred roasted red bell pepper, well drained

1 tablespoon extra-virgin olive oil (see Tips)

2 teaspoons fresh lemon juice

1 clove garlic, minced, or ½ teaspoon prepared minced garlic

1 teaspoon sugar

¼ teaspoon freshly ground pepper, or to taste

⅛ teaspoon salt, or to taste

Process all the ingredients in a blender or food processor until the mixture is smooth. Taste and adjust the seasoning.

ADVANCE PREPARATION
This sauce will keep for up to 3 days in a tightly closed container in the refrigerator.

TIPS

Extra-virgin olive oil, the most flavorful and expensive of olive oils, is made from the first pressing of top-quality olives. It has a full-bodied, fruity taste and low acidity. It is the best choice for use in uncooked dishes or to add for flavor in the final stages of cooking. "Olive oil" or "pure olive oil" is a more-refined and less-flavorful olive oil. It is used for cooking, because the flavor of extra-virgin oil dissipates somewhat when heated. Olive oils vary according to growing areas, grade, and quality; color tells little about them. Conduct your own taste test to find the one you like best.

Store all olive oils in a cool, dark place and use within 1 year. Refrigerate the oil during hot weather; it will become thick and cloudy but this does not affect the flavor or quality. Simply bring the oil to room temperature before using to restore the clarity.

Apricot, Pear, and Apple Chutney

MAKES 2 CUPS

THIS SWEET CHUTNEY COMPLEMENTS CHEESE. A KEY COMPONENT IN CREAM CHEESE AND CHUTNEY TRAMEZZINI (PAGE 46), IT IS GREAT ON THE SIDE WHEN YOU SERVE OPEN-FACED BREAKFAST SANDWICHES (PAGE 91) OR WITH THIS SIMPLE CHEESE SANDWICH: SPREAD TOASTED BAGELS WITH DIJON MUSTARD, TOP WITH SLICES OF PEPPER JACK, AND BROIL UNTIL BUBBLY AND LIGHTLY BROWNED.

TIPS

ZESTING CITRUS RIND: Zesting is done with a kitchen gadget called a zester, which has a short, flat blade with a beveled end and 5 small holes. When drawn firmly over the rind of citrus fruit, the zester removes thin strips of the colored skin. (Do not strip off the white part beneath; it has a bitter flavor.) You can also use a vegetable peeler to remove strands of the colored skin, then use a small knife to cut them into thinner strips.

GRATING CITRUS RIND: Use a handheld fine grater, which will reduce the skin to tiny particles.

1 1/2 cups finely diced apple (about 1 medium apple)

1/4 cup coarsely chopped dried apricots, loosely packed (about 8 apricot halves)

1/4 cup dried cranberries

1 tablespoon lemon zest (see Tips)

1/4 cup fresh lemon juice

3 tablespoons white rice vinegar

3 tablespoons water

1 tablespoon packed light brown sugar

1/2 teaspoon ground cinnamon

1/8 teaspoon freshly ground pepper

Salt to taste

1 1/2 cups finely diced pear (about 1 medium pear)

ADVANCE PREPARATION
This chutney will keep for up to 1 week in a covered container in the refrigerator. Serve chilled, at room temperature, or reheat, stirring gently.

Put all the ingredients except the pear in a medium saucepan. Cover and cook over medium-high heat until the liquid comes to a boil. Reduce the heat to medium and continue to cook, covered, stirring occasionally, for about 10 minutes. Stir in the pear; cook, covered, stirring occasionally, until all the fruits are tender, about 5 more minutes. Remove from the heat and let cool.

VARIATIONS
Substitute other dried fruits, such as apples or raisins (up to 1/2 cup), for the apricots and cranberries.

Substitute other fresh fruits, such as a peach, mango, or pineapple (up to 3 cups total) for the apple and pear.

Apricot-Orange Sauce

MAKES ⅓ CUP

USE THIS CONCENTRATED FRUITY SAUCE IN SESAME-SOY MUSHROOMS ON CROSTINI (PAGE 35) AND ASIAN ROASTED VEGETABLE WRAPS (PAGE 109). ADD THE RED PEPPER FLAKES IF YOU WANT A TOUCH OF HOTNESS TO COMPLEMENT THE SWEETNESS.

¼ cup loosely packed coarsely chopped dried apricots (about 8 apricot halves)

½ cup fresh orange juice

¼ teaspoon minced fresh ginger (see Tips)

Dash of red pepper flakes, or to taste (optional)

ADVANCE PREPARATION
This sauce will keep for up to 4 days in a covered container in the refrigerator; bring to room temperature before using.

Put the apricots and orange juice in a small saucepan. Cover and bring the liquid to a boil over medium-high heat. Reduce the heat to low; simmer until the apricots are very soft, about 4 minutes.

Transfer the mixture to a blender or food processor; process until it is thick and smooth. Stir in the ginger and the red pepper flakes, if using. Taste and adjust the seasoning.

Bagel Crisps

1 BAGEL MAKES 6 BAGEL CRISPS

WHEN YOU HAVE A CONTAINER OF HUMMUS (PAGE 17), MARINATED GOAT CHEESE (PAGE 23), OR SUN-DRIED TOMATO PESTO (PAGE 15) IN YOUR REFRIGERATOR, MAKE SOME BAGEL CRISPS. A CRUNCHY GOURMET TREAT IS JUST MINUTES AWAY. TRY THESE FOR SNACKS, APPETIZERS, AND AS A CRISP ACCOMPANIMENT TO SOUPS OR SALADS.

---

1 or more bagels, preferably flavored (such as an onion or sun-dried tomato)

Preheat the oven to 375°F. Cut each bagel into six ¼-inch-thick horizontal slices. Place the slices in a single layer on a baking sheet.

ADVANCE PREPARATION
Bagel crisps will keep for up to 1 week in a covered tin at room temperature.

Toast the slices in the oven for about 5 minutes, turning once, or until they are lightly browned on both sides and crispy.

TIPS

When buying mature fresh ginger, look for a piece that is firm, with smooth brown skin and no soft spots. Peel before using, if you like. Mince ginger well so the flavor will be distributed evenly in the dish.

To store ginger: If stored at room temperature, fresh ginger will keep only a few days. For longer storage, wrap the ginger tightly in aluminum foil or seal in a small self-sealing plastic bag and freeze. When you need ginger, simply use a fine grater to grate off the amount needed. Rewrap and replace in the freezer, where the ginger will keep for up to 3 months.

Jars of minced ginger are available in most produce departments; check the labels, since some products also contain garlic and sweeteners. Dried ginger does not have the same distinctive flavor and should not be substituted for fresh in recipes.

These attractive small sandwiches rely on fresh herbs, vegetables, and fruits in perfect pairings: fragrant basil with juicy tomatoes, peppery watercress with cool cucumbers, roasted beets drenched in hazelnut oil, portobello mushrooms with apricots, sweet pear slices and herbed goat cheese. You might serve a colorful assortment and forget dinner altogether.

Many of these sandwiches can be made in advance. For others, a simple last-minute sautéing, toasting, or broiling will fill your kitchen with enticing aromas.

Since these sandwiches are small and light, serve them to your guests as appetizers and to your family as snacks. As an accompaniment to a soup or salad, they will add an extra dimension to complete a meal. And they make a light meal when your time is limited or if you want an effortless but satisfying meal for one.

BRUSCHETTA AND CROSTINI

While traveling in Italy, two culinary staples stand out in my memory: bruschetta and crostini. Quite simply, these are toasts, traditionally toasted over a wood-burning fire to add a smoky flavor.

Bruschetta is thick slices of country French or Italian bread; crostini are smaller, less filling versions of bruschetta, made from thinner slices of French baguette.

In Italy, crostini are often served in restaurants as an antipasto preceding a meal or with aperitifs, and trattorias transform bruschetta into a quick lunch by embellishing the toasts with a wide variety of fragrant and colorful toppings. What makes them outstanding are the combinations of just a few top-quality ingredients—such as brilliant red sun-ripened tomatoes (the best I have ever tasted), vibrant green fresh basil, and aromatic extra-virgin olive oil—all atop artisan breads. American chefs, too, have embraced the seasonless bruschetta, often using non-Italian toppings.

Bruschetta and crostini can be served unadorned right after toasting, or you can add your choice of topping. If you wish, toast the bread early in the day and complete the creations just before serving. Here are the basic recipes, accompanied by suggestions for several of my favorite toppings, some traditional, others novel pairings.

Bruschetta

½- to ¾-inch-thick slices plain rustic Italian or French bread (day-old, if you like)

Halved garlic cloves for rubbing, or Roasted Garlic (page 25) for spreading

Extra-virgin olive oil for drizzling

Salt and freshly ground pepper to taste (optional)

Preheat the broiler. Or the bread can be toasted on the stove on a dry stovetop grill pan or over a charcoal fire. If you are using a broiler, arrange the bread slices in a single layer on a baking sheet. Broil or grill the bread slices on both sides until they are golden brown and crisp on the outside, yet still chewy and not dry on the inside.

Rub one side of each warm slice with cut garlic; the more you rub, the stronger the flavor. Or, spread the warm toasts with roasted garlic. Drizzle lightly or brush the same side with plain or flavored extra-virgin olive oil. Sprinkle with salt and freshly ground pepper, if desired.

Crostini

⅜-inch-thick slices French baguette

Olive oil, as needed

Preheat the oven to 400°F. Lightly brush olive oil on both sides of each bread slice. Arrange the slices in a single layer on a baking sheet. Bake for about 2 minutes per side, or until the toasts are golden brown but not firm all the way through.

BRUSCHETTA and CROSTINI TOPPINGS

Toppings that don't require additional broiling can be spooned into a bowl to accompany a basket of the toasts. Your guests can then assemble their own at the table. Spread toasts with:

Roasted Garlic (page 25).

Guacamole (page 18) and top with fresh cilantro sprigs.

Hummus (page 17) and top with thin tomato slices.

Marinated Goat Cheese (page 23) and top with strips of **Roasted Red Bell Pepper** (page 26), chopped drained oil-packed sun-dried tomatoes, or **toasted pine nuts** or **walnuts** (see pages 37 and 89).

Basil Pesto (page 16), sprinkle with freshly ground pepper, and top with shredded mozzarella cheese; broil just until the cheese melts.

Black Olive-Tomato Spread (page 62); broil just long enough to soften the cheese.

Tomato and Basil Bruschetta or Crostini

MAKES 8 BRUSCHETTAS OR 16 CROSTINI; SERVES 4

THIS CLASSIC DUO IS A STAPLE IN ITALY, WHERE ONLY THE BEST INGREDIENTS WILL DO.

TIP

Roma (plum) tomatoes, have thick, meaty walls, small seeds, little juice, and a rich, sweet flavor. They are the best choice for recipes that benefit from less juicy tomatoes that retain their shape after being chopped or sliced.

TOPPING

2 Roma (plum) tomatoes, finely diced (about 1 cup); see Tip

1 tablespoon extra-virgin olive oil

2 cloves garlic, minced, or 1 teaspoon prepared minced garlic

1/4 teaspoon freshly ground pepper, or to taste

8 large basil leaves

2 tablespoons freshly grated Parmesan cheese

8 Bruschettas (page 33)
or
16 Crostini (page 33)

ADVANCE PREPARATION
This topping will keep for up to 1 day in a covered container in the refrigerator. Bring the topping to room temperature; assemble and broil the sandwiches just before serving.

TO MAKE THE TOPPING: Stir all the ingredients except the basil and Parmesan cheese together in a small bowl.

Preheat the broiler. Place the bruschettas or crostini in a single layer on a baking sheet. Arrange the basil leaves on the toasted bread. Top with the tomato mixture; sprinkle with the cheese. Broil the sandwiches 4 to 5 inches from the heat source for about 2 minutes, or until the cheese is melted. Serve warm or at room temperature.

VARIATION
Tear the basil leaves into smaller pieces and toss together with the tomato mixture.

Sesame-Soy Mushrooms with Apricot-Orange Sauce on Crostini

MAKES 16 CROSTINI; SERVES 4

BE PREPARED FOR PRAISE. THESE CROSTINI ARE INTRIGUING AND COLORFUL.

SESAME-SOY MUSHROOMS

Sixteen ½-inch-thick slices portobello mushroom caps (about 2 large mushroom caps)

2 tablespoons soy sauce

2 tablespoons Asian sesame oil (see Tips)

2 tablespoons canola oil (see Tips)

1 teaspoon sugar

⅓ cup Apricot-Orange Sauce (page 29) or bottled Chinese plum sauce

16 Crostini (page 33)

16 stemmed arugula leaves

Toasted sesame seeds (see Tip, page 44) for garnish

TO MAKE THE SESAME-SOY MUSHROOMS:

Preheat the broiler. Arrange the mushroom slices in a single layer on a baking sheet. Combine the soy sauce, oils, and sugar in a small bowl; stir until the sugar is dissolved. Brush this seasoning sauce on the tops of the mushroom slices; broil 4 to 5 inches from the heat source for 2 minutes. Turn the mushroom slices and brush the other side with the seasoning sauce (reserve the remaining sauce); broil for about 2 more minutes, or until the mushrooms are tender. Watch closely; they cook quickly. Set aside and keep warm.

Spread about 1 teaspoon of the apricot-orange or plum sauce on each toast; top with an arugula leaf and a mushroom slice. Drizzle each sandwich with a small amount of the soy seasoning sauce; garnish with sesame seeds. Serve warm or at room temperature.

TIPS

Buy dark, amber-colored Asian sesame oil, made from toasted sesame seeds, rather than light-colored sesame oil, which is extracted from raw sesame seeds and lacks the distinctive strong, nutty flavor. Purchase Asian sesame oil in the Asian section of supermarkets or in Asian markets. After opening, store it in the refrigerator, where it will keep for up to 6 months.

Canola oil is a neutral oil that allows the other flavors in the recipe to shine through. For example, recipes with Asian flavors provided by soy sauce, Asian sesame oil, and ginger call for a neutral cooking oil. Store canola oil in the refrigerator.

Bell Pepper Bruschetta or Crostini

MAKES 4 BRUSCHETTAS OR 8 CROSTINI; SERVES 4

IF YOU HAVE SUN-DRIED TOMATO PESTO (PAGE 15), MARINATED GOAT CHEESE (PAGE 23),
OR FRESH GOAT CHEESE ON HAND, SPREAD A LAYER ON THE TOASTS BEFORE ADDING
THIS SWEET, SEDUCTIVE TOPPING.

TOPPING
1 tablespoon olive oil

½ cup thinly sliced red onion

½ red bell pepper, seeded, deveined, and
cut into ⅛-inch-wide strips

½ yellow bell pepper, seeded, deveined, and
cut into ⅛-inch-wide strips

2 cloves garlic, minced, or
1 teaspoon prepared minced garlic

2 teaspoons red wine vinegar (see Tips)

Salt and freshly ground pepper to taste

4 Bruschettas (page 33)
or
8 Crostini (page 33)

Freshly grated Parmesan cheese
and/or toasted pine nuts (see Tips) for garnish

ADVANCE PREPARATION
*This topping will keep for up to 1 day
in a covered container in the refrigerator;
bring to room temperature before using.*

TO MAKE THE TOPPING: Heat the olive oil in a large nonstick skillet over medium-high heat. Add the onion; cook, stirring occasionally, until nearly tender, about 4 minutes. Add the bell peppers and garlic; continue to cook, stirring constantly, until the vegetables are tender, about 5 more minutes. Remove the pan from the heat and stir in the vinegar, salt, and pepper. Taste and adjust the seasoning.

Top the bruschettas or crostini with the bell pepper mixture. Garnish with the cheese and nuts, and serve warm or at room temperature.

TIPS

Wine vinegars, produced from the acetic fermentation of wine, are mellow in flavor and retain the aroma of the wine from which they are made. Most vinegars will keep for up to 2 years without refrigeration. Some, especially red wine vinegars, may become cloudy or develop a sediment. If this happens, the flavor will not be affected; the liquid can be cleared by running it through a paper coffee filter.

Pine nuts (also called *pignoli*) are the seeds from the cone of certain pine trees. Their natural oil turns rancid very quickly, so they should be refrigerated for no more than 1 month or frozen for up to 3 months in a tightly closed container.

TOASTING PINE NUTS: The sweet, mild flavor of pine nuts is enhanced by toasting. Put the pine nuts in a small dry skillet over medium heat; stir constantly and watch carefully until the nuts are lightly browned, about 4 to 5 minutes. Or, preheat the oven to 375°F. Spread a single layer of nuts on an ungreased baking sheet; bake for 4 to 5 minutes, stirring frequently. Immediately remove the nuts from the pan as soon as they are browned. I usually toast 1 cup at a time and then freeze the nuts until I need them.

Spinach and Carrot Bruschetta or Crostini

MAKES 4 BRUSCHETTAS OR 8 CROSTINI; SERVES 4

THIS TOPPING BOASTS STUNNING COLORS AND IS GOOD FOR YOU, TOO.

TIPS

Packaged spinach, often labeled "salad spinach," sold in most supermarkets, consists of tender, young, delicately flavored spinach leaves that have been washed before packaging. Before using bunched spinach, be sure to rinse the leaves under cold running water to remove any sand, then dry. Remove and discard the stems before using spinach.

Spinach will keep for up to 4 days if stored in a sealed plastic bag in the refrigerator vegetable crisper. If the leaves seem wilted, wrap them in moist paper towels and refrigerate to revive.

To shred spinach, roll a stack of the leaves cigar style, and then cut by hand with a large knife.

TOPPING

1 tablespoon olive oil

1 carrot, coarsely shredded (about ½ cup)

2 cloves garlic, minced, or
1 teaspoon prepared minced garlic

3 cups coarsely shredded stemmed spinach leaves (see Tips)

1 teaspoon fresh lemon juice

Salt and freshly ground pepper to taste

4 Bruschettas, made without garlic (page 33)
or
8 Crostini (page 33)

2 tablespoons freshly shredded Romano cheese

Toasted pine nuts (see Tip, page 37) for garnish

TO MAKE THE TOPPING: Heat the olive oil in a large nonstick skillet over medium-high heat. Add the carrot and garlic; cook, stirring constantly, until the carrot is tender, about 2 minutes. Add the spinach; cook, stirring constantly, until it is wilted, about 1 more minute. Remove the pan from the heat. Stir in the lemon juice, salt, and pepper. Taste and adjust the seasoning.

Spread the spinach topping on the bruschettas or crostini. Sprinkle with the cheese and garnish with pine nuts. Serve warm.

White Bean and Swiss Chard Bruschetta

MAKES 8 BRUSCHETTAS; SERVES 4

IT'S BEST TO TOAST THE BREAD FOR THIS SANDWICH ON A GRILL AND THEN
RUB THE BRUSCHETTA WITH FRESH GARLIC. SERVE THE SANDWICHES WARM OR AT ROOM
TEMPERATURE AS APPETIZERS, OR AS ACCOMPANIMENTS TO SOUP OR SALAD
(TRY GREENS TOSSED WITH HALVED CHERRY TOMATOES, BLACK OLIVES, FETA CHEESE, AND
LEMON VINAIGRETTE, PAGE 24).

WHITE BEAN SPREAD
1 tablespoon olive oil

One 15-ounce can white beans or
navy beans, drained and rinsed

1/2 cup water

2 cloves garlic, minced, or
1 teaspoon prepared minced garlic

2 teaspoons minced fresh sage, or
1/2 teaspoon dried sage

1/4 teaspoon freshly ground pepper, or to taste

Salt to taste

TOPPING
2 tablespoons olive oil

4 cups finely shredded stemmed Swiss chard leaves
(see Tips)

1/2 cup finely chopped onion

2 cloves garlic, minced, or
1 teaspoon prepared minced garlic

1 tablespoon red wine vinegar

1/8 teaspoon red pepper flakes, or to taste

Salt and freshly ground pepper to taste

8 Bruschettas (page 33)

Toasted pine nuts (see Tip, page 37) for garnish

TO MAKE THE SPREAD: Heat the olive oil in a medium nonstick skillet over medium-high heat. Add the beans, water, garlic, and sage; cook, stirring occasionally and mashing, until the mixture forms a paste, about 5 minutes. Add the pepper and salt. Taste and adjust the seasoning. Remove from the heat and set aside; cover if you plan to serve the sandwiches warm.

TO MAKE THE TOPPING: Heat the olive oil in a nonstick skillet. Add the chard, onion, and garlic; cook, stirring constantly, until the greens are wilted and the onion is tender, about 5 minutes. Remove from the heat. Stir in the vinegar, red pepper flakes, salt, and pepper. Taste and adjust the seasoning. Cover if you plan to serve the sandwiches warm.

Spread the bean mixture on the bruschettas; top with greens and sprinkle with pine nuts. Serve warm or at room temperature.

VARIATION
Substitute kale (see Tips) for the Swiss chard.

TIPS

Swiss chard is a member of the beet family. Red chard, with its dark green leaves and reddish stalks, has a stronger flavor than varieties with lighter colored leaves and stalks. Chard is available year-round, but the best quality is found during the summer.

Kale is a member of the cabbage family. Ornamental varieties come in shades of blue and purple; for cooking, choose dark green kale. Store it in the coldest section of the refrigerator for no longer than 2 or 3 days; after that, the flavor becomes quite strong and the leaves turn limp. Because the center stalk is tough, remove it before cooking.

Pear Crostini

MAKES 8 CROSTINI; 4 SERVINGS

SERVE THIS IN THE WINTER WHEN THE BEST PEARS ARE AVAILABLE. ALLOW TIME FOR RIPENING (YOU WILL WANT TO BUY THEM AHEAD), BUT REMEMBER THAT SLIGHTLY UNDERRIPE PEARS ARE THE BEST FOR COOKING AND BAKING.

PEAR TOPPING

1 large pear at room temperature, cored and halved lengthwise (see Tip)

1 tablespoon pure maple syrup

8 Crostini (page 33)

1/4 cup Marinated Goat Cheese (page 23) or garlic and herb-flavored goat cheese

3 tablespoons freshly grated Parmesan cheese

TO MAKE THE TOPPING: Cut each pear half crosswise into twelve 1/4-inch-thick slices. Toss the pear slices and maple syrup in a small bowl. Let stand at room temperature for about 10 minutes to allow the flavors to blend.

Preheat the broiler. Arrange the crostini in a single layer on a baking sheet. Spread each toast with goat cheese. Use a slotted spoon to strain the pear slices; arrange a row of 3 overlapping slices on each toast. Sprinkle with Parmesan cheese. Broil the crostini 4 to 5 inches from the heat source for about 1 1/2 to 2 minutes, or until the pear slices are tender and the cheese is melted and lightly browned. Serve warm or at room temperature.

VARIATION

Substitute cashew butter for goat cheese.

Roasted Beet Crostini

MAKES 4 BRUSCHETTAS OR 8 CROSTINI; SERVES 4

BEFORE STORING THE BEETS, REMOVE THE GREENS (SEE TIP); BUT BE SURE TO KEEP THEM,
SINCE THEY ARE AN ESSENTIAL INGREDIENT IN THIS RECIPE. ROASTING DRAWS FORTH BEETS' NATURAL
SWEETNESS. ADD THE EXQUISITE FLAVOR OF HAZELNUT OIL, AND THE COMBINATION
IS SUBLIME.

HAZELNUT VINAIGRETTE

2 tablespoons hazelnut oil

2 tablespoons red wine vinegar

1/2 teaspoon Dijon mustard

1/8 teaspoon freshly ground pepper

Dash of salt

ROASTED BEET TOPPING

4 red beets, peeled and cut into
1/4-inch-thick slices (see Tip)

2 tablespoons olive oil

1/4 cup coarsely chopped red onion

2 cups coarsely shredded stemmed beet greens

4 Bruschettas (page 33) or 8 Crostini (page 33)

1/3 cup Marinated Goat Cheese (page 23) or
fresh white goat cheese

Freshly ground pepper to taste

ADVANCE PREPARATION

*The beets can be roasted up to 2 days in advance
and stored in a sealed container in the refrigerator.
Because the greens may discolor after cooking,
cook them and assemble the sandwiches
just before serving.*

TO MAKE THE VINAIGRETTE: Whisk all the ingredients together in a small bowl.

TO MAKE THE TOPPING: Preheat the broiler. Toss the beet slices with 1 tablespoon of the olive oil in a small bowl. Spread the slices in a single layer on a baking sheet. Broil 4 to 5 inches from the heat source, turning once, for about 15 to 20 minutes, or until they are fork-tender. Let cool.

Meanwhile, heat the remaining 1 tablespoon olive oil in a medium nonstick skillet over medium-high heat. Add the onion; cook, stirring occasionally, until tender, about 3 minutes. Add the greens; cook, stirring constantly, until they are wilted, about 1 minute. Remove the pan from the heat.

Cut the beet slices into 1/4-inch-wide strips. (First, cover your work surface with waxed paper and don disposable plastic gloves to prevent staining.) Whisk the vinaigrette, then stir it and the beets into the greens. Let cool.

Spread the toasts with marinated or fresh white goat cheese; top with the beet mixture and sprinkle with pepper. Serve warm or at room temperature.

Choose small to medium firm beets with smooth skins and crisp greens. They draw moisture from the root, so remove the greens (except for an inch or two of the stems) when you get them home from the market. Store the nutritious, delicious greens in a perforated plastic bag in the refrigerator for up to 3 days. The beets will keep in a plastic bag in the refrigerator for up to 1 week.

Sesame-Herb Crostini

MAKES 12 CROSTINI; SERVES 4

THESE CROSTINI WERE INSPIRED BY A POPULAR ISRAELI APPETIZER.
YOU MAY SERVE THE YOGURT IN A SMALL BOWL, SPRINKLED WITH THE TOPPING, SO YOUR GUESTS
CAN HELP THEMSELVES, USING SMALL COCKTAIL KNIVES TO SPREAD THE TOPPING
ONTO THEIR CROSTINI.

----

12 Crostini (page 33)

1/2 clove garlic for rubbing, or as desired

Rub one side of each warm toast slice with the cut side of the garlic clove; the more you rub, the stronger the flavor.

SESAME-HERB TOPPING
1 teaspoon toasted sesame seeds (see Tips)

1/4 teaspoon dried summer savory

1/8 teaspoon cayenne

1/8 teaspoon ground cumin

1/8 teaspoon salt

TO MAKE THE TOPPING: Combine the sesame seeds, summer savory, cayenne, cumin, and salt in a small bowl.

3/4 cup Yogurt Cheese (page 22)

6 green olives, thinly sliced

2 teaspoons extra-virgin olive oil

Spread each toast slice with about 1 tablespoon yogurt cheese; sprinkle with some of the sesame seed mixture. Arrange a few olive slices on each toast, then drizzle with a small amount of olive oil.

VARIATION
Omit the olive slices; increase the salt in the topping to 1/4 teaspoon.

ADVANCE PREPARATION
Prepare the topping up to 1 week in advance; store it in a covered container at room temperature. Assemble the crostini just before serving.

TIPS

Because they contain oil, sesame seeds will become rancid at room temperature; store them in an airtight container in the refrigerator for up to 6 months or in the freezer for up to 1 year.

TOASTING SESAME SEEDS:
Toasting gives sesame seeds a slightly crispy texture and a nutty flavor. Put the sesame seeds in a dry skillet over medium-high heat and toss or stir constantly for about 3 to 5 minutes, or until they are lightly browned. Or, spread the seeds on an ungreased baking sheet and bake in a preheated 350°F oven; shake the pan or stir occasionally for about 10 minutes. Once they are toasted, immediately remove the seeds from the skillet or baking sheet. It takes the same amount of time to toast 1 tablespoon or 1/2 cup, so toast extra seeds, store them in an airtight container, and refrigerate or freeze.

Cremini Mushroom–Toasted Almond Spread on Bagel Crisps

MAKES 6 SANDWICHES; SERVES 6

THIS HEALTHY APPETIZER IS A HIT IN MY SPA COOKING CLASSES.
CRUNCHY BAGELS ARE THE PERFECT COMPLEMENT TO THE SOFT-TEXTURED MUSHROOM SPREAD,
WHICH IS RICH-TASTING WITHOUT BEING HEAVY. I LIKE TO USE ONION-FLAVORED OR
SUN-DRIED TOMATO BAGELS.

CREMINI MUSHROOM–TOASTED ALMOND SPREAD

2 tablespoons olive oil

2 cups (10 ounces) sliced cremini mushrooms (see Tips)

¼ cup minced shallots (see Tips)

1 teaspoon minced fresh tarragon, or ¼ teaspoon dried tarragon

¼ cup toasted sliced almonds (see Tip, page 89)

2 teaspoons fresh lemon juice

2 teaspoons soy sauce

Ground white pepper to taste (see Tips)

6 Bagel Crisps (page 29)

Strips of Roasted Red Bell Pepper (page 26) or fresh red bell pepper strips and fresh tarragon sprigs for garnish

ADVANCE PREPARATION
For the best flavor, make this spread the day before serving. It will keep for up to 4 days in a covered container in the refrigerator. Bring to room temperature before serving.

TO MAKE THE SPREAD: Heat the oil in a large nonstick skillet over medium-high heat. Add the mushrooms and shallots; cook, stirring occasionally, until the mushrooms are tender, about 5 minutes. Remove the pan from the heat; stir in the dried tarragon (if using). Let cool slightly, then transfer the mixture to a food processor. Add the almonds, lemon juice, soy sauce, and pepper; process until the mixture is smooth. Stir in the fresh tarragon (if using). Taste and adjust the seasoning.

Spread about 2 tablespoons of the mushroom mixture on each bagel crisp. Garnish and serve at room temperature.

TIPS

Cremini mushrooms (sometimes labeled "Italian brown mushrooms") are more flavorful and have a denser, less watery texture than ordinary white mushrooms; portobello mushrooms are larger, matured cremini.

Shallots, a member of the onion family, are small bulbous herbs with a mild onion-garlic flavor. Always use fresh shallots; dehydrated products have an inferior flavor. (If fresh are unavailable, substitute some fresh onion and fresh garlic.) Store shallots for up to 1 month in the bottom bin of your refrigerator; use them before they begin to sprout. Don't allow shallots to brown as they cook, or they will taste bitter.

The berries of the pepper vine are used to produce both black and white pepper. For black pepper, green berries are picked and sun-dried, turning black and shrinking in the process. For white pepper, the berries are ripened on the vine; then they are picked and soaked in water to remove the outer coating, leaving the inner gray-white kernel. These kernels are sun-dried to produce white pepper. White pepper is slightly less spicy than black pepper.

Many of my favorite lunchtime memories are of eating tramezzini at elegant wine and espresso bars throughout Italy. These thin sandwiches are made with a fine-textured white bread called *pane in cassetta,* similar to our white sandwich bread.

The creations are quite simple, so you can use your imagination to create appetizing variations. It's fun to set out a platter with an array of tramezzini. Serve them as a light lunch or with drinks before dinner.

To create your own tramezzini, select white sandwich bread cut into thin slices (about ¼ inch thick); trim the crusts off the bread for a more refined appearance. Spread a condiment on the bread for moisture and flavor. This can be as simple as a plain or flavored mayonnaise (page 21), or Sun-Dried Tomato Pesto (page 15) or Black Olive and Caper Spread (page 19). Use only one or two main ingredients in the sandwich filling to keep the sandwiches thin.

For authentic tramezzini, add typically Italian ingredients, such as thin slices of fresh mozzarella cheese, tomatoes, mushrooms, strips of Roasted Red Bell Peppers (page 26), and a layer of fresh greens such as arugula, basil, or radicchio. Or create your own combinations, using non-Italian ingredients, with spreads such as Guacamole (page 18), Hummus (page 17), or Yogurt Cheese (page 22).

If the tramezzini are made in advance, refrigerate the sandwiches in plastic wrap or drape a slightly dampened dish towel over them and refrigerate for up to 2 hours before serving.

Cream Cheese and Chutney Tramezzini

MAKES 2 SANDWICHES; SERVES 2

MAKE APRICOT, PEAR, AND APPLE CHUTNEY (PAGE 28)
IN ADVANCE OR USE MANGO CHUTNEY FROM THE SUPERMARKET.

4 slices white sandwich bread, crusts removed

2 tablespoons cream cheese or Yogurt Cheese (page 22) at room temperature

2 tablespoons chutney

Fresh watercress sprigs (thick stems removed), as desired (see Tip)

Spread one side of each bread slice with the cream cheese or yogurt cheese. Spread 2 bread slices with a layer of chutney and add several watercress sprigs. Top with the remaining 2 bread slices, cream cheese–side down, and slice each sandwich diagonally or into 4 strips to form finger sandwiches.

VARIATION
Substitute fresh white goat cheese for the cream cheese and stemmed arugula leaves for the watercress.

Cucumber and Watercress Tramezzini

MAKES 2 SANDWICHES; SERVES 2

PEPPERY WATERCRESS IS ESPECIALLY TASTY WITH CUCUMBER.
THE PAIRING REMINDS ME OF SANDWICHES SERVED AT TEATIME IN ENGLAND. HERE, HOWEVER,
THE WATERCRESS IS MIXED WITH YOGURT TO MAKE A ZESTY SAUCE.

TIP

Refrigerate hot pepper sauce after opening to retain its flavor and red color.

WATERCRESS-YOGURT SAUCE

¼ cup plain yogurt

2 tablespoons minced fresh watercress

⅛ teaspoon dry mustard

Pinch of sugar, or to taste

Salt and freshly ground pepper to taste

2 drops hot pepper sauce, or to taste (see Tip)

4 slices white sandwich bread, crusts removed

One 3-inch chunk cucumber, cut into twelve ⅛-inch-thick slices

Salt to taste

TO MAKE THE SAUCE: Stir all the ingredients together in a small bowl. Taste and adjust the seasoning.

Spread one side of each bread slice with the yogurt sauce. Arrange a layer of cucumber slices on 2 of the bread slices; lightly sprinkle with salt. Top with the remaining 2 bread slices, sauce-side down. Slice the sandwiches diagonally once or twice.

Egg and Radish Tramezzini

MAKES 2 SANDWICHES; SERVES 2

*THESE VERY SIMPLE SANDWICHES ARE AMONG MY FAVORITES; I LIKE THE FRESH CRUNCH
AND BRIGHT PEPPERY FLAVOR OF THE RADISH.*

4 slices white sandwich bread, crusts removed

Garlic Mayonnaise (page 21), as desired

2 hard-cooked eggs,
cut into ¼-inch-thick slices (see Tip, page 67)

Salt (see Tips) and freshly ground pepper to taste

2 large radishes, cut into ⅛-inch-thick slices

Snipped fresh chives

Thin strips of green onion tops (see Tips)

Fresh watercress sprigs
(thick stems removed), as desired

Spread one side of each bread slice with the mayonnaise. Top 2 bread slices with a layer of half of the egg slices; lightly sprinkle with salt and pepper. Top each bread slice with half the radish slices and chives, green onion, and watercress, if using. Top with the remaining bread slices. Cut each sandwich in half diagonally once or twice.

VARIATION
Substitute cucumber slices for the radish slices.

My preference is to use sea salt. It has a fuller flavor, so less is usually needed. You can purchase sea salt in many supermarkets as well as in natural foods stores. Fine sea salt can be used just like ordinary table salt. Coarse sea salt can be finely ground in a salt mill for use in recipes or at the table. (Make sure that the salt mill has a stainless steel or other noncorrosive mechanism.)

Green onions, also called scallions or spring onions, are delicately flavored members of the onion family. The size varies from very slender to large and thick; as a rule, the more slender the bottoms, the sweeter the flavor. The leaves should be bright green and firm; the white bulbs should be firm and unblemished. Both parts can be used in recipes calling for green onions. Wrap green onions in a plastic bag and store them for up to 1 week in the vegetable crisper section of the refrigerator.

Blue Cheese and Apple Spread on Cocktail Rye

MAKES 12 SANDWICHES; SERVES 4

SERVE THESE LITTLE OPEN-FACED APPETIZER SANDWICHES ON AUTUMN EVENINGS
WHEN THE ROBUST FLAVORS SEEM ESPECIALLY APPROPRIATE. FOR A LIGHT LUNCH OR DINNER,
PAIR THEM WITH HERBED FRESH TOMATO-CARROT SOUP (PAGE 120) AND A GREEN SALAD
TOSSED WITH LEMON VINAIGRETTE (PAGE 24).

The strong flavor and aroma of blue cheese intensifies with aging. Commonly available varieties include Danablu, Gorgonzola, Roquefort, and Stilton.

TIP

The strong flavor and aroma of blue cheese intensifies with aging. Commonly available varieties include Danablu, Gorgonzola, Roquefort, and Stilton.

---

12 slices cocktail rye bread

Preheat the broiler. Arrange the bread slices in a single layer on a baking sheet; broil 4 to 5 inches from the heat source until the tops are firm, about 2 minutes.

BLUE CHEESE AND APPLE SPREAD

½ cup cream cheese at room temperature

½ cup (2 ounces) crumbled blue cheese (see Tip)

½ cup diced red apple

2 tablespoons coarsely chopped toasted walnuts (see Tip, page 89)

2 tablespoons fresh lemon juice

1 tablespoon minced fresh tarragon, or 1 teaspoon dried tarragon

TO MAKE THE SPREAD: Stir the cream cheese and blue cheese together in a medium bowl; take care not to mash the blue cheese. Gently stir in all the remaining topping ingredients.

Top each toasted bread slice with about 1 tablespoon blue cheese–apple mixture. Serve at room temperature. If you prefer, broil the sandwiches for about 2 minutes, or until the topping is warm, then serve immediately.

ADVANCE PREPARATION

This topping will keep for up to 2 days in a covered container in the refrigerator. Bring to room temperature and assemble the sandwiches just before serving.

VARIATION

Substitute ½ cup halved red seedless grapes for the apple; serve at room temperature (do not broil).

COLD sandwiches

Many of these sandwiches are do-ahead favorites. Make some of the spreads and fillings in advance, as well as an accompaniment from the Sandwich Accompaniments chapter (pages 111 to 121), so that you can get a hearty lunch or dinner on the table in a hurry.

The Vegetarian Pan Bagnat (page 57) makes a fine lunch on the go. Take Focaccia with Creamy Vegetable Spread (page 63) to your next picnic. The Dilled Egg Salad Sandwiches with Vegetables (page 67) satisfy a hungry family on busy Saturday afternoons. And put the Open-Faced Crispy Tortilla Sandwiches (page 61) and the Sweet Potato and Avocado Sandwiches with Tahini–Poppy Seed Spread (page 58) on your menus for lunchtime guests.

These creations are stacked to the max, so purchase a box of frilly sandwich picks to hold layers together. You'll also want some colorful heavy-duty napkins.

East Indian Tea Sandwiches

MAKES 2 SANDWICHES; SERVES 2

MY FRIEND RAGHAVAN IYER SHARED THIS RECIPE WITH ME ALONG WITH HIS FOND MEMORIES OF EATING THIS SANDWICH AT PICNICS IN HIS HOMETOWN, BOMBAY. THE CILANTRO-PEANUT SPREAD IS A ZESTY COMPLEMENT TO THE COOLING FLAVORS OF THE CUCUMBER AND POTATO IN THE FILLING. FOR MORE INTENSITY, ADD AN EXTRA THAI CHILE; FOR A LESS ASSERTIVE FLAVOR, SUBSTITUTE A JALAPEÑO OR SERRANO. HERE, AS IN BOMBAY, THIS SANDWICH IS IDEAL FOR A MIDSUMMER PICNIC. MY FAVORITE NONTRADITIONAL ACCOMPANIMENT IS RED PEPPER AND GREEN APPLE RELISH WITH CILANTRO VINAIGRETTE (PAGE 119) OR A SWEET PICKLE OR TWO.

CILANTRO-PEANUT SPREAD
1/4 cup fresh cilantro leaves

1 Thai chile, coarsely chopped (see Tip, page 80)

1/4 cup plain yogurt

1 tablespoon unsalted dry-roasted peanuts

1 teaspoon minced fresh ginger

Salt to taste

1 red boiling potato

4 slices white potato bread, crusts removed

Four 1/4-inch-thick tomato slices

Salt and freshly ground pepper to taste

1/4 cucumber, peeled and cut into eight 1/4-inch-thick diagonal slices (see Tip)

Two 1/8-inch-thick red onion slices

TO MAKE THE SPREAD: Process all the ingredients in a food processor until the peanuts are finely chopped but not puréed. Taste and adjust the seasoning.

Cook the potato in salted boiling water until fork-tender, about 15 minutes. Drain and rinse with cold water, then drain again. Let cool, then cut into eight 1/4-inch-thick slices.

Lightly toast the bread slices. Spread one-fourth of the peanut spread on each bread slice. Top each slice with half of the potato and tomato slices; sprinkle with salt and pepper. Top each bread slice with a layer of half of the cucumber and onion slices. Top each sandwich with another bread slice, spread-side down, and cut it in half twice diagonally to form 4 triangles.

ADVANCE PREPARATION
This spread will keep for up to 2 days in a covered container in the refrigerator. Assemble the sandwiches up to 1 hour before serving; if held longer, the toasted bread will soften.

TIP

Many cucumbers are sold with a waxy coating to prolong their shelf life; unfortunately, the wax also seals in pesticides. The only way to remove the wax is by peeling. Better yet, buy unwaxed cucumbers. The elongated European cucumbers (sometimes called hothouse or English cucumbers) are usually the better choice. They are grown hydroponically (in water) without pesticides. They have an excellent, mild flavor, a more tender texture, and fewer seeds. Store unwashed whole cucumbers in a plastic bag in the refrigerator for up to 10 days; once cut, seal in plastic wrap and refrigerate for up to 5 days.

Vegetarian Pan Bagnat

MAKES 2 SANDWICHES; SERVES 2

PAN BAGNAT BEGAN AS A FRENCH *SALADE NIÇOISE* WITH CROUTONS. HERE, I'VE TRADED THE TUNA AND ANCHOVIES FOR PROTEIN-RICH EGGS AND BEANS. TO MULTIPLY THE RECIPE, ARRANGE THE INGREDIENTS IN A HORIZONTALLY SLICED LOAF OF FRENCH BREAD, THEN CUT DIAGONALLY TO FORM SINGLE SERVINGS.

TIP

Fava beans (also called broad beans and horse beans) look like very large, dark-skinned lima beans. In supermarkets, they may be found fresh in spring-time, still in their large, green pods (only about 4 to 6 to a pod), and they can be purchased dried or in cans year round. Fava beans are popular in Mediterranean and Middle Eastern dishes.

VINAIGRETTE
2 tablespoons extra-virgin olive oil

1 tablespoon red wine vinegar

1 clove garlic, minced, or
½ teaspoon prepared minced garlic

½ teaspoon Dijon mustard

½ teaspoon sugar

Salt and freshly ground pepper to taste

One 6-inch diameter round plump country bread roll (such as a French boule), sliced horizontally

FILLING
½ cup canned fava beans, drained and rinsed (see Tip)

½ cucumber, peeled and cut into ⅛-inch-thick slices

½ green bell pepper, seeded, deveined, and cut into ¼-inch-wide strips

¼ cup small black olives (preferably niçoise), pitted and halved

One 2-ounce can pimientos, drained and cut into thin strips

4 thin red onion slices

2 hard-cooked eggs, cut into ¼-inch-thick slices (see Tip, page 67)

Freshly ground pepper to taste

1 tomato, cut into ¼-inch-thick slices

About 6 large basil leaves, torn

TO MAKE THE VINAIGRETTE: Whisk all the ingredients together in a small bowl. Taste and adjust the seasoning.

Remove some of the soft bread from inside the roll. Brush the cut surfaces with the vinaigrette.

TO MAKE THE FILLING: Combine the beans, cucumber, bell pepper, olives, and pimientos in a medium bowl; toss with the remaining vinaigrette.

Spoon the bean mixture into the bottom bread shell. Top with the onion and egg slices; sprinkle with pepper. Add the tomato slices and basil leaves. Top with the other bread shell, press gently, and wrap tightly with several layers of plastic wrap. Refrigerate for at least 1 hour.

If possible, let the sandwich stand at room temperature for half an hour before serving (or wrap in plastic and refrigerate for up to 4 hours). Use a serrated knife to slice the roll in half to make 2 sandwiches.

VARIATIONS
Add or substitute other typical Provençal ingredients, such as artichoke hearts, celery hearts, roasted red bell peppers, mushrooms, capers, and greens.

Spread the bread with fresh white goat cheese or add crumbled feta or thin slices of mozzarella cheese.

Sweet Potato and Avocado Sandwiches with Tahini–Poppy Seed Spread

MAKES 2 SANDWICHES; SERVES 2

SWEET POTATOES ARE A SURPRISE HERE. WITHOUT EXCEPTION, EVERYONE WHO TASTES THIS SANDWICH RAVES ABOUT THE DELECTABLE COMBINATION OF TASTES. COLORFUL AND FLAVORFUL, THIS SANDWICH IS ONE OF MY FAVORITES, ESPECIALLY WHEN ACCOMPANIED WITH A JUICY TUSCAN PEPPERONCINI (SEE TIPS).

TIPS

Pepperoncini are thin chile peppers usually sold pickled; the slightly sweet flavor can range from medium to medium-hot.

Tahini, a paste made made by grinding sesame seeds, is also called sesame butter or sesame paste. Although it is high in fat, the flavor is concentrated, so a little goes a long way. Light tahini is preferable to the more intensely flavored dark tahini, which is made from toasted sesame seeds. Stir before using to reincorporate the oil. You can store tahini for up to 1 year in a tightly closed container in the refrigerator.

The distinction between yams and sweet potatoes is confusing; what is labeled a "yam" at the supermarket most likely is an "orange sweet potato." Orange sweet potatoes have a dark, uniformly colored brown to purplish skin, a shape that tapers on both ends, an orange flesh, and a sweet flavor when cooked. White sweet potatoes have a lighter skin, yellow flesh, and a delicately spicy, less sweet flavor. Store sweet potatoes in a cool, dark, dry place for up to 1 week; do not refrigerate.

TAHINI–POPPY SEED SPREAD

1 tablespoon tahini (see Tips)

1 tablespoon plain yogurt

2 teaspoons fresh lemon juice

½ teaspoon honey

¼ teaspoon poppy seeds

1 small orange-fleshed sweet potato (about 7 ounces), peeled and cut into 2-inch-thick slices (see Tips)

4 slices whole-wheat bread

Four ⅛-inch-thick red onion slices

½ small avocado, peeled, pitted, and cut into ¼-inch-thick slices

Four ¼-inch-thick tomato slices

Salt and freshly ground pepper to taste

¼ cup shredded Monterey jack cheese

Finely shredded lettuce or alfalfa sprouts, as desired (see Tip, page 71)

ADVANCE PREPARATION

This spread will keep for up to 3 days in a covered container in the refrigerator. The sweet potato can be cooked early the day it is to be served; cover and refrigerate. Assemble the sandwiches just before serving.

TO MAKE THE SPREAD: Whisk all the ingredients together in a small bowl.

Cook the sweet potato slices in salted boiling water until fork-tender, about 15 minutes. Drain and rinse with cold water, then drain again. Let cool, then cut the slices into six ¼-inch-thick slices.

Lightly spread the tahini mixture on one side of 2 bread slices. Top each slice with half of the onion, avocado, and tomato slices; sprinkle lightly with salt and pepper. Add a layer of half of the sweet potato slices, cheese, and lettuce or sprouts. Top with the remaining 2 bread slices. Slice the sandwiches in half. Fasten each half with a decorative sandwich pick.

VARIATIONS

Substitute Guacamole (page 18) for the Tahini–Poppy Seed Spread; omit the additional avocado.

Rather than boiling the sweet potato slices, steam them over boiling water in a covered pot for 8 to 10 minutes. Or, cook the whole potato in the microwave: Pierce several holes in the skin of the potato with a fork. Microwave on high for about 8 minutes, or until it is fork-tender, then peel and slice.

A canned sweet potato (not "candied") can be substituted for the fresh sweet potato.

Open-Faced Crispy Tortilla Sandwiches

MAKES 2 SANDWICHES; SERVES 2

SERVE THESE ELEGANT OPEN-FACED CRISPY SANDWICHES FOR A LIGHT LUNCH. THE PROCEDURE MAY APPEAR LENGTHY, BUT THE INDIVIDUAL COMPONENTS CAN BE PREPARED EARLY IN THE DAY, EVEN IF THE RECIPE IS MULTIPLIED. (AS A TIMESAVER, SUBSTITUTE BOTTLED ROASTED RED BELL PEPPER SAUCE AVAILABLE IN THE GOURMET SECTION OF MOST SUPERMARKETS.) QUICKLY ASSEMBLE THE COLORFUL SANDWICHES JUST BEFORE SERVING.

TIP

Fresh mozzarella, available at an Italian market, cheese store, or the specialty cheese section of the supermarket, is a soft white cheese with a delicate texture and mild flavor, and is very different from the type of mozzarella often used on pizza.

Two 7-inch flour tortillas

2 teaspoons olive oil

TOPPING

1 tablespoon olive oil

3/4 cup diced red bell pepper

3/4 cup diced yellow bell pepper

3/4 cup diced green bell pepper

1/2 cup diced peeled zucchini

1/4 cup minced red onion

2 cloves garlic, minced, or 1 teaspoon prepared minced garlic

1 tablespoon fresh lemon juice

Dash of salt and freshly ground pepper to taste

1/4 cup Black Olive and Caper Spread (page 19)

3 ounces fresh mozzarella cheese; cut into 1/2-inch cubes (1/2 cup); see Tip

1/2 cup Roasted Red Bell Pepper Sauce (page 27)

Fresh watercress or basil sprigs for garnish

Preheat the broiler. Cut each tortilla into 4 wedges; lightly brush both sides with olive oil. Place the tortillas on a baking sheet and prick the surfaces in several places with a fork. Broil 4 to 5 inches from the heat source for about 1 to 2 minutes on each side, or until lightly browned. Watch closely! Set aside on a plate; they will become crisper as they cool.

TO MAKE THE TOPPING: Heat the oil in a medium nonstick skillet over medium-high heat. Add the bell peppers, zucchini, onion, and garlic. Cook, stirring occasionally, until the bell peppers are tender, about 8 to 10 minutes. Remove from the heat; stir in the lemon juice, salt, and pepper. Taste and adjust the seasoning.

Spoon some of the olive spread onto each of the tortilla wedges. Top with the bell pepper mixture and dot with the cheese. Arrange on a serving plate, drizzle with the red bell pepper sauce, and garnish. Provide generously sized napkins and eat the sandwiches with your fingers.

VARIATIONS

Substitute 1/4 cup Basil Pesto (page 16) for the Black Olive and Caper Spread.

Substitute 1/2 cup Guacamole (page 18) for the Black Olive and Caper Spread and substitute 1/4 cup fresh white goat cheese for the fresh mozzarella; omit the Roasted Red Bell Pepper Sauce.

Grilled Eggplant with Black Olive–Tomato Spread on Focaccia

MAKES 8 SANDWICHES; SERVES 8

A GREAT PARTY SANDWICH TO CHARM THE MOST SOPHISTICATED PALATES, THIS LOOKS IMPRESSIVE SERVED ON AN ATTRACTIVE LARGE, ROUND PLATTER. FOR A CROWD, CUT ROUND FOCACCIA INTO EIGHT WEDGES OR INTO THINNER PIECES FOR APPETIZER SERVINGS. OFFER BOWLS OF MARINATED OVEN-DRIED TOMATOES (PAGE 114), HAZELNUT–GREEN BEAN SALAD (PAGE 113), AND MARINATED ANY-BEAN SALAD (PAGE 115) ON THE SIDE.

TIP

To remove the bitter flavor from a large, mature eggplant, slice the eggplant, sprinkle both sides of the slices liberally with coarse salt, and let the slices drain in a colander for 30 to 60 minutes. Rinse the slices and squeeze them dry between paper towels before using the eggplant in a recipe. This procedure is not necessary if you are using young, smaller eggplants. The peel of eggplants is edible, so it is not necessary to remove it before cooking; peel it for the sake of appearance or texture. Store eggplants for up to 2 weeks in a plastic bag in the refrigerator; keep the stem on until just before using.

BLACK OLIVE–TOMATO SPREAD

One 4-ounce can chopped ripe black olives

¼ cup tomato paste

2 tablespoons cream cheese, Yogurt Cheese (page 22), fresh white goat cheese, or Marinated Goat Cheese (page 23)

2 tablespoons red wine vinegar

2 teaspoons minced fresh oregano, or ½ teaspoon dried oregano

2 cloves garlic, minced, or 1 teaspoon prepared minced garlic

¼ teaspoon freshly ground pepper

2 tablespoons olive oil

1 tablespoon fresh lemon juice

Dash of salt and freshly ground pepper to taste

1 eggplant (about 1 pound), peeled and cut into ½-inch-thick crosswise slices (see Tip)

One 10-inch round or square sun-dried tomato, onion, or rosemary focaccia, halved horizontally

12 large stemmed spinach leaves

1 large tomato, cut into ¼-inch-thick slices

ADVANCE PREPARATION

This spread will keep for up to 5 days in a covered container in the refrigerator.

TO MAKE THE SPREAD: Process all the ingredients in a food processor until nearly smooth.

Prepare an outdoor grill for cooking. Combine the olive oil, lemon juice, salt, and pepper in a small bowl. Brush one side of the eggplant slices with the mixture. Arrange them, oiled-sides down, on a grill rack about 6 inches from medium-hot coals. Cook for about 4 minutes; brush the tops with the olive oil mixture, then turn. Cook for about 4 more minutes, or until the slices are tender and lightly browned. Transfer the grilled eggplant to a plate and let cool.

Spread half of the black olive–tomato mixture on each cut side of the focaccia. Arrange the spinach leaves on the bottom half. Top with a layer of tomato slices and then eggplant slices. Sprinkle with salt and pepper. Top with the second focaccia half and press gently. Use a serrated knife to slice the focaccia into 8 wedges or squares just before serving.

VARIATION

Cook the eggplant slices on a stovetop grill pan (see Tip, page 86), preferably nonstick, or on a baking sheet under a preheated broiler for about 4 minutes per side.

Focaccia with
Creamy Vegetable Spread

MAKES 8 SANDWICHES; SERVES 8

THIS SANDWICH TRAVELS WELL, SO IT'S GREAT FOR PICNICS OR LUNCH ON THE GO. WRAP THE SANDWICH IN PLASTIC AND REFRIGERATE FOR AT LEAST 1 HOUR BEFORE SERVING. THE CHEESE WILL BECOME FIRMER, MAKING THE SANDWICH EASIER TO EAT; THE FLAVORS WILL HAVE A CHANCE TO BLEND, TOO. TAKE ALONG HAZELNUT–GREEN BEAN SALAD (PAGE 113) OR MARINATED ANY-BEAN SALAD (PAGE 115).

CREAMY VEGETABLE SPREAD

½ cup (4 ounces) fresh white goat cheese at room temperature

½ cup (4 ounces) cream cheese at room temperature

¼ cup freshly grated Parmesan cheese (see Tips)

2 cloves garlic, minced, or 1 teaspoon prepared minced garlic

2 Roasted Red Bell Peppers (page 26) or jarred roasted red bell peppers, well drained, coarsely chopped

1 Roma (plum) tomato, diced (about ½ cup)

One 6 ½-ounce jar marinated artichoke hearts, drained and coarsely chopped

¼ cup minced red onion

2 tablespoons minced fresh basil

Dash of salt and freshly ground pepper to taste

One 10-inch round or square plain focaccia, halved horizontally

Freshly ground pepper to taste

ADVANCE PREPARATION

This spread will keep for up to 3 days in a covered container in the refrigerator. The assembled and wrapped sandwich can be refrigerated for up to 8 hours before serving.

TO MAKE THE SPREAD: Process the 3 cheeses and the garlic in a food processor until nearly smooth. Toss all the remaining spread ingredients in a small bowl. Stir in the cheese mixture. Taste and adjust the seasoning.

Place the bottom of the focaccia on a cutting board; spread the cut side of the bottom with the cheese mixture. Sprinkle with pepper. Top with the second focaccia half and press gently.

Wrap the sandwich in plastic wrap and refrigerate for at least 1 hour. Use a serrated knife to slice it into 8 wedges or squares just before serving.

VARIATION

Add or substitute other vegetables (up to 1½ cups total) to the spread, such as drained and chopped oil-packed sun-dried tomatoes or shredded carrots.

TIPS

Use a hand grater or food processor to grate your own cheese from a block of Parmesan just before using or purchase freshly grated Parmesan at a cheese shop or deli. Commercially packaged grated domestic Parmesan cheese, sold unrefrigerated, is loaded with preservatives, has the consistency of sawdust, and is overly salty.

The best-quality Parmesan cheese is Italy's Parmigiano-Reggiano. It is usually aged 3 to 4 years, which results in a granular texture and complex flavor compared with domestic varieties that are aged for about 1 year. The imported cheese also melts well.

Sealed in a tightly closed container, grated Parmesan will keep in the refrigerator for up to 1 week. It can be frozen; however, the flavor and texture will deteriorate. Wrapped tightly in plastic wrap and refrigerated, a block of Parmesan will keep for up to 4 weeks.

Roasted Red Pepper–Avocado Clubs
with White Bean Hummus

MAKES 2 SANDWICHES; SERVES 2

I LIKE THE FLAVOR AND APPEARANCE OF BUTTER-CRUST BREAD FOR THIS SANDWICH,
BUT YOUR FAVORITE WHITE LOAF IS JUST FINE. SELECT AN UNSLICED LOAF OF BREAD AND
ASK THE BAKERY TO CUSTOM-CUT IT INTO $1/4$-INCH-THICK SLICES.

Eight thin (about $1/4$-inch-thick) slices white bread, preferably butter-crust

FILLING

$1/3$ cup White Bean Hummus (page 17)

1 Roasted Red Bell Pepper (page 26) or jarred roasted red bell pepper, well drained, cut into 1-inch-wide strips

$1/2$ avocado, peeled, pitted, and cut into $1/4$-inch-thick slices

$1/2$ tomato, cut into $1/4$-inch-thick slices (see Tips)

2 tender lettuce leaves, such as red leaf lettuce

Lightly toast the bread in a toaster.

Spread 1 heaping tablespoon of hummus on one side of each of the bread slices. Top each of 2 slices of the bread, hummus-side up, with half of the roasted red bell pepper strips, then top each with a slice of bread, hummus-side up. Top each with a layer of half of the avocado slices. Top each with another slice of bread, hummus-side up. Top each with a layer of tomato slices, then a lettuce leaf. Top each with a slice of bread, hummus-side down. Press gently and halve each sandwich diagonally. Fasten each half with a decorative sandwich pick.

VARIATION

If you are unable to find thinly sliced bread, use 3 slices of regular sandwich bread for each sandwich. Layer from the bottom up as follows: bread, hummus, red bell pepper, bread, hummus, tomato, avocado, lettuce, hummus, bread.

Dilled Egg Salad Sandwiches with Vegetables

MAKES 2 SANDWICHES; SERVES 2

KEEP A CONTAINER OF THE EGG SALAD ON HAND IN THE REFRIGERATOR FOR ON-THE-SPOT AFTER-SCHOOL SNACKS. OR TRY THIS ELEGANT APPETIZER: SPREAD THE EGG SALAD ON SLICES OF COCKTAIL-SIZED CARAWAY RYE OR ROUNDS OF GRAINY BREAD; OMIT THE LETTUCE OR SPROUTS AND GARNISH THE OPEN-FACED SANDWICHES WITH SMALL SPRIGS OF FRESH DILL.

DRESSING

2 tablespoons plain yogurt or mayonnaise

2 teaspoons snipped fresh dill, or ¼ teaspoon dried dill

1 teaspoon Dijon mustard

1 teaspoon fresh lemon juice

¼ teaspoon honey

½ clove garlic, minced, or ¼ teaspoon prepared minced garlic

Salt and freshly ground pepper to taste

3 hard-cooked eggs (see Tips)

2 tablespoons minced carrot

2 tablespoons minced green bell pepper

1 tablespoon minced celery

1 tablespoon minced red onion

1 tablespoon capers, drained and rinsed

4 slices rye bread

Mayonnaise and mustard for spreading

2 large tomato slices

Finely shredded lettuce or alfalfa sprouts, as desired (see Tip, page 71)

ADVANCE PREPARATION

The egg salad will keep for up to 2 days in a tightly closed container in the refrigerator.

TO MAKE THE DRESSING: Stir all the ingredients together in a small bowl.

Mash the eggs with a fork. Add the carrot, bell pepper, celery, onion, and capers; toss. Stir in the dressing. Taste and adjust the seasoning. Spread one side of 2 slices of bread with mayonnaise and one side of the other 2 slices with mustard.

Spread the egg salad mixture over the mayonnaise on 2 of the bread slices. Add a tomato slice and lettuce or sprouts to each. Top each sandwich with another slice of bread, mustard-side down, and cut in half.

TIPS

Store uncooked eggs in the carton, large ends up, in the coldest part of your refrigerator (not in the refrigerator door) for up to 1 month. (But for the best flavor, use them within 1 week.)

HARD-COOKING EGGS: Place the eggs in a single layer in a medium pan and cover with at least 1 inch of cold water. Cover and bring the water to a full rolling boil over medium-high heat. Remove the pan from the heat and let the eggs stand in the water, covered, for about 15 minutes for large eggs. (For larger or smaller eggs, adjust the time up or down by about 3 minutes for each size variation.) Drain off the hot water and immediately cover the eggs with cold water; let stand until the eggs are completely cool. This cooling process prevents a dark gray-green surface from forming around the yolk. (If it does occur, the greenish color is harmless and does not alter the nutritional value or flavor of the egg.) Quick cooling also causes eggs to contract, making them easier to peel. Refrigerate hard-cooked eggs for up to 1 week.

WARM sandwiches

Substantial warm sandwiches stand on their own. Made with vegetables—steamed, sautéed, roasted, and grilled—eggs, cheese, and beans, they are spread between tortillas, heaped on focaccia and English muffins, layered between slices of bread, spooned into croissants, and stuffed into onion rolls or hoagie and hamburger buns. Use your favorite whole-grain and rye breads, and a sun-dried tomato bread from your neighborhood artisan bread shop.

Try Croissants Stuffed with Herbed Scrambled Eggs, Spinach, Apples, and Brie (page 92) and Omelet Focaccia Sandwiches (page 95) for the main event at brunch. Burger fans will flip over Portobello Mushroom Burgers (page 90) and Savory Nut Patties on Sesame Buns (page 89), two-fisted kid-food for grownups. Open-faced sandwiches, such as Baked Asparagus Toast with Zesty Cheese Sauce, (page 79) Mushroom-Shallot Croustades (page 76), and Veggie Melts (page 71) call for knives and forks for easier eating.

The spreads and sauces used in these sandwiches can be prepared in advance, so plan to make them ahead and stock up.

These sandwiches are meant to be served warm, so time the final steps so you can serve them just as soon as they are prepared.

Veggie Melts

MAKES 2 SANDWICHES; SERVES 2

THESE OPEN-FACED SANDWICHES REQUIRE A SHARP KNIFE AND A FORK FOR GRACIOUS EATING.
OFFER MARINATED OVEN-DRIED TOMATOES (PAGE 114), AND LUNCH IS COMPLETE.

(PAGE 114)

2 slices cracked wheat bread

Mayonnaise for spreading

TOPPING

1 tablespoon olive oil

1 cup (5 ounces) sliced mushrooms

1/2 cup coarsely shredded zucchini (see Tips)

1/2 cup finely sliced onion

1 clove garlic, minced, or 1/2 teaspoon prepared minced garlic

Salt and freshly ground pepper to taste

1/4 cup finely shredded Monterey jack cheese

1/4 cup finely shredded Cheddar cheese

Four 1/2-inch-thick tomato slices

Finely shredded lettuce or fresh bean sprouts, as desired (see Tips)

Preheat the broiler. Arrange the bread slices in a single layer on a baking sheet. Broil 4 to 5 inches from the heat source for about 2 minutes per side, or until lightly toasted. Or, toast the bread in a toaster. Spread one side of each slice with mayonnaise.

TO MAKE THE TOPPING: Heat the olive oil in a large nonstick skillet over medium-high heat; add the mushrooms, zucchini, onion, and garlic. Cook, stirring occasionally, until tender, about 5 minutes. Remove from the heat, stir in the salt and pepper. Taste and adjust the seasoning.

Combine the cheeses in a small bowl. Top each bread slice with 2 tomato slices, a sprinkling of pepper to taste, and half of the sautéed vegetables, lettuce or bean sprouts, and cheese mixture.

Place the sandwiches on the baking sheet. Broil for about 2 minutes, or until the cheese is melted.

TIPS

Do not choose zucchini that are not firm or with skin that is cut, bruised, dull, or shriveled; small zucchini are more tender. Like other squashes, zucchini are 95 percent water, so cook them quickly or they will become mushy.

Sprouts make a fresh, tasty, and crunchy addition to sandwiches. However, a recent study suggests that raw sprouts may sometimes be contaminated with bacteria. The FDA (Food and Drug Administration) recommends that the elderly, small children, and those with weak immune systems should avoid eating raw sprouts. In case this is a concern to you, I have offered the alternative of using finely shredded lettuce, rather than sprouts, in some of the sandwiches.

Grilled Portobello Mushroom Sandwiches with Sun-Dried Tomato and Goat Cheese Spread

MAKES 2 SANDWICHES; SERVES 2

PORTOBELLOS ARE IDEAL FOR GRILLING. THESE IMMENSE MUSHROOMS ACHIEVE THEIR SIZE THROUGH A LONG GROWING CYCLE. IN THE PROCESS, SOME OF THE MUSHROOMS' MOISTURE EVAPORATES, CONCENTRATING AND ENRICHING THE FLAVOR, AND CREATING A DENSE, MEATY TEXTURE.

SUN-DRIED TOMATO AND GOAT CHEESE SPREAD
2 tablespoons minced oil-packed sun-dried tomatoes

2 tablespoons fresh white goat cheese at room temperature

1 tablespoon red wine vinegar

1 tablespoon extra-virgin olive oil

1 clove garlic, minced, or ½ teaspoon prepared minced garlic

Pinch of sugar

Pinch of red pepper flakes, or to taste

Salt to taste

2 large portobello mushroom caps

Two ¼-inch-thick red onion slices

Olive oil for brushing

Salt and freshly ground pepper to taste

2 crusty French onion rolls, halved horizontally

2 tablespoons freshly grated Parmesan cheese, or 2 very thin slices provolone cheese

8 arugula leaves (see Tip)

ADVANCE PREPARATION
This spread will keep for up to 5 days in a covered container in the refrigerator. Grill the vegetables and assemble the sandwiches just before serving.

TO MAKE THE SPREAD: Process all the ingredients in a food processor until the mixture is nearly smooth. Taste and adjust the seasoning.

Prepare an outdoor grill for cooking. Brush the rounded tops of the mushrooms and the onion slices with olive oil. Arrange them, oiled sides down, on the grill rack about 6 inches from medium-hot coals. Cook for about 3 minutes; brush the other side with additional oil, then turn. Cook for about 3 more minutes, or until tender and lightly browned. Transfer to a plate and sprinkle lightly with salt and pepper. Cover to keep warm.

Spread the sun-dried tomato mixture on the cut sides of each roll. Add cheese to the bottom half of each roll, then top with the following layers: arugula leaves, onion slices, and a mushroom cap. Top with the upper half of the rolls. Fasten each sandwich with long sandwich picks and slice in half.

VARIATIONS
Substitute Marinated Goat Cheese (page 23), Basil Mayonnaise (page 21), or Sun-Dried Tomato Pesto (page 15) for the Sun-Dried Tomato and Goat Cheese Spread.

Cook the mushroom caps and onions on a stovetop grill pan or under a preheated broiler for 3 to 4 minutes per side. Substitute toasted sandwich buns for the crusty onion rolls.

Baked Avocado and Cheese Sandwiches

MAKES 2 SANDWICHES; SERVES 2

My local bread shop's sun-dried tomato bread, loaded with bits of tomato and lots of flavor, inspired this sandwich; rye or whole wheat bread would also do well. Accompany the sandwiches with Herbed Fresh Tomato-Carrot Soup (page 120) to make the meal complete.

Poppy seeds provide a crunchy texture and nutty flavor. Because of their high oil content, they are prone to rancidity; store poppy seeds in an airtight container for up to 6 months in the refrigerator.

Foil sheets sized for wrapping sandwiches are available in most supermarkets.

SPREAD
2 tablespoons Garlic Mayonnaise (page 21)

1 tablespoon horseradish mustard, or to taste

2 teaspoons minced onion

½ teaspoon poppy seeds (see Tips)

4 slices sun-dried tomato bread

Four ¼-inch-thick slices smoked Cheddar, mozzarella, or Gouda cheese (about 4 ounces)

Four ¼-inch-thick avocado slices

Four ¼-inch-thick tomato slices

Freshly ground pepper to taste

Preheat the oven to 350°F.

TO MAKE THE SPREAD: Stir all the ingredients together in a small bowl.

Generously spread one side of each bread slice with the mayonnaise mixture. Layer with slices of cheese, avocado, and tomato; lightly sprinkle with pepper. Top with the remaining 2 bread slices, spread-side down.

Wrap each sandwich in aluminum foil (see Tips). Place the sandwiches on a baking sheet and heat in the oven for about 15 minutes, or until the cheese is melted.

Eggplant-Parmesan Poor Boys

MAKES 4 SANDWICHES; SERVES 4

TO SPEED UP THE PREPARATIONS FOR THESE SANDWICHES, USE A JAR OF YOUR FAVORITE MEATLESS SPAGHETTI SAUCE. MY FAVORITE IS TOMATO-BASIL, AND I ADD A PINCH OF RED PEPPER FLAKES FOR A LITTLE ZEST

One 14-ounce jar marinara sauce

EGGPLANT-PARMESAN FILLING
1 egg

1 tablespoon water

½ cup packaged herb and garlic-seasoned dried bread crumbs

2 tablespoons olive oil

½ eggplant (about 8 ounces), peeled and cut into twelve ¼-inch-thick crosswise slices

Four 6- to 8-inch poor boy (sub or hoagie) buns, halved horizontally

Mayonnaise, preferably Garlic Mayonnaise (page 21) or Basil Mayonnaise (page 21) for spreading

2 cups coarsely shredded stemmed spinach leaves

½ cup (2 ounces) freshly grated Parmesan cheese

VARIATION
Spread the buns with Marinated Goat Cheese (page 23) instead of mayonnaise.

Preheat the oven to 375°F. Heat the marinara sauce in a small saucepan over medium heat, stirring occasionally.

TO MAKE THE FILLING: Beat the egg lightly in a shallow bowl; stir in the water. Pour the bread crumbs into a separate shallow bowl. Heat 1 tablespoon of the oil in a large nonstick skillet over medium heat until a drop of water bubbles when dropped in. Dip several eggplant slices, one at a time, into the egg, then press both sides into the bread crumbs. Cook until browned on the bottom; turn and cook until browned on the second side and tender, about 4 to 5 minutes per side. As you remove the slices from the skillet, place them on a paper towel–covered plate and cover to keep warm. Repeat with the remaining eggplant slices, adding the remaining 1 tablespoon oil as needed, until all are cooked.

While cooking the last batch of eggplant slices, arrange the buns, cut-sides up, on a baking sheet and toast in the oven for about 4 minutes, or until the cut surfaces are lightly browned.

Spread mayonnaise on the cut surfaces of each bun. Layer each bottom half with spinach and 3 overlapping eggplant slices. Drizzle with marinara sauce and sprinkle with Parmesan cheese. Top each sandwich with an upper bun half, mayonnaise-side down.

Mushroom-Shallot Croustades

MAKES 8 SANDWICHES; SERVES 4

CROUSTADES ARE EDIBLE CONTAINERS; HERE, THEY ARE MADE FROM BREAD SLICES THAT ARE FORMED INTO LITTLE CUPS WHEN THEY ARE TOASTED IN MUFFIN TINS. YOU'LL FIND THAT IT'S EASIER TO WORK WITH BREAD THAT IS VERY FRESH AND MOIST. SERVE 2 OF THESE CROUSTADES WITH A CREAMY TOPPING WITH A GREEN SALAD FOR A LIGHT MEAL, OR 1 TO EACH GUEST AS A FIRST COURSE.

----

8 thin slices (about ¼-inch thick) fresh white bread

FILLING

½ cup vegetable stock (see Tips)

¼ cup heavy cream

2 tablespoons dry sherry (see Tips)

2 tablespoons butter

2 cups (10 ounces) sliced cremini or white mushrooms

2 tablespoons minced shallot

1 tablespoon flour

2 teaspoons minced fresh thyme, or ½ teaspoon dried thyme

⅛ teaspoon freshly ground pepper, or to taste

Salt to taste

Snipped fresh chives for garnish

Preheat the oven to 350°F. Use a large round cookie cutter or knife to cut the bread slices into 3-inch rounds. Gently press the rounds into muffin cups. Bake for about 10 minutes, or until the bread shells are lightly browned.

TO MAKE THE FILLING: Stir the vegetable stock, cream, and sherry together in a measuring cup; set aside. Melt the butter in a medium nonstick skillet over medium-high heat. Add the mushrooms and shallot; cook, stirring constantly, until the mushrooms are tender, about 4 minutes. Reduce the heat to medium-low; add the flour and stir constantly for about 1 minute. Gradually add the stock mixture and cook, stirring constantly and scraping the bottom of the pan, until the sauce is smooth and thickened, about 2 minutes. Remove from the heat; stir in the thyme, pepper, and salt. Taste and adjust the seasoning.

Remove the toasts from the tins and place them on a baking sheet. Spoon 1 heaping tablespoon of the mushroom and sauce mixture into each toast shell. Heat the croustades in the oven for about 3 minutes. Garnish each filled shell with the chives and provide forks.

TIPS

Vegetable stock can be made using vegetable stock powder, cubes, or concentrates, all of which are available in natural foods stores. Check the label for an unsalted product, free of flavor enhancers and preservatives.

Sherry is wine to which brandy has been added to increase the flavor and alcohol content. Sherries vary in color, flavor, and sweetness. Finos are dry and light; manzanillas are very dry, delicate finos with a hint of saltiness. Olorosos, often labeled cream or golden sherry, are darker in color and sweet. Avoid using cooking sherry, which is inferior in flavor and overly salty.

Baked Asparagus Toast with Zesty Cheese Sauce

MAKES 4 SANDWICHES; SERVES 4

SERVE THESE OPEN-FACED SANDWICHES WITH APPLE-CRANBERRY SALAD (PAGE 116) OR FRUIT.

ZESTY CHEESE SAUCE
2 tablespoons butter

2 tablespoons flour

1 cup milk

1 cup (4 ounces) finely shredded Cheddar cheese (see Tips)

1/2 teaspoon dry mustard

Salt to taste

1/8 teaspoon cayenne, or to taste (see Tips)

4 slices whole-wheat bread or 2 whole-wheat English muffins, halved

Mustard for spreading

FILLING
12 asparagus spears (16 or 20 if the asparagus is very thin)

1 tablespoon butter

1 tablespoon olive oil

3 cups (15 ounces) sliced cremini mushrooms

Four 1/2-inch-thick tomato slices

Dash of sweet paprika, preferably Hungarian

Preheat the oven to 350°F. Lightly coat an 8-by-10-inch baking pan with cooking spray.

TO MAKE THE SAUCE: Melt the butter in a medium nonstick saucepan over medium heat. Add the flour and stir constantly until the mixture is smooth and bubbly. Gradually add the milk, whisking constantly until the sauce is smooth and thickened, about 3 minutes. Reduce the heat to low; add the remaining sauce ingredients. Stir constantly until the cheese is melted. Remove from the heat. Taste and adjust the seasoning. Cover and set aside.

Arrange the bread or English muffin halves in a single layer in the baking pan. Toast in the oven for about 2 minutes, or until the top surfaces are lightly browned. Lightly spread each with mustard.

TO MAKE THE FILLING: Steam the asparagus over boiling water in a covered pot for about 4 minutes, or until crisp-tender. Drain well.

Melt the butter with the oil in a medium nonstick skillet over medium-high heat; add the mushrooms. Cook, stirring occasionally, until tender, about 5 minutes.

Top each bread slice or muffin half with a tomato slice. Add a layer of mushrooms and asparagus spears to each. Pour the cheese sauce over sandwiches; sprinkle with paprika. Bake the sandwiches for about 8 minutes, or until the cheese sauce is bubbly.

TIPS

Firm, semifirm, and semisoft cheeses should be wrapped airtight in a plastic bag; store in the refrigerator cheese compartment (or warmest location) for up to several weeks. Mold may be cut away if it develops. Fresh and soft-ripened cheeses should be tightly wrapped; they will keep in the coldest part of the refrigerator for up to 2 weeks. Discard fresh or soft-ripened cheeses that become moldy. All cheeses taste best if served at room temperature.

Cayenne is the ground dried pod of small, more pungent varieties of chilies. Use with caution, because it is very hot. Store it in a tightly closed container in the refrigerator to retain its color and flavor.

Black Bean Quesadillas

MAKES 12 SMALL TORTILLA SANDWICHES; SERVES 4

SANDWICHED BETWEEN 2 TORTILLAS, BLACK BEANS AND VEGETABLES ARE SPICED UP WITH A HOT PEPPER. SERVE THESE SKINNY, WARM GRILLED-CHEESE MEXICAN SANDWICHES WITH A GREEN SALAD OR RED PEPPER AND GREEN APPLE RELISH WITH CILANTRO VINAIGRETTE (PAGE 119) FOR A LIGHT LUNCH. FOR AN APPETIZER OR SOUP ACCOMPANIMENT, LET THE QUESADILLAS COOL AND CUT THEM INTO SMALLER WEDGES.

The hotness of chilies depends on the amount of a substance called capsaicin (kap-SAY-ih-sihn), found mainly in the veins and seeds. Capsaicin retains its potency despite time, cooking, or freezing, so removing the veins and seeds before using peppers is the only way to reduce the heat. Small peppers have more membranes and seeds than large peppers, so generally they are hotter. To avoid irritation from the caustic oils in chile peppers, do not touch your eyes, nose, or lips while handling them. Many cooks wear disposable plastic gloves when working with hot chilies. Afterward, wash your hands, knife, and cutting board in hot, soapy water.

FILLING

1 tablespoon olive oil

2 bell peppers (use a mixture of red, yellow, orange, or green bell peppers), seeded, deveined, and finely chopped (about 2 cups)

1/4 cup finely chopped onion

1 jalapeño chile, minced (about 1 tablespoon); see Tips

1 clove garlic, minced, or 1/2 teaspoon prepared minced garlic

1/2 cup canned black beans, drained and rinsed

1/2 cup coarsely chopped Roma (plum) tomato

2 tablespoons sliced black olives

1 tablespoon red wine vinegar

2 teaspoons minced fresh oregano, or 1/2 teaspoon dried oregano

1/8 teaspoon freshly ground pepper, or to taste

Salt to taste

Four 7-inch flour tortillas

1 cup (4 ounces) coarsely shredded Monterey jack cheese

Sour cream for garnish

ADVANCE PREPARATION

The quesadilla filling will keep for up to 3 days in a covered container in the refrigerator. Bring to room temperature; assemble and bake the quesadillas just before serving.

Preheat the oven to 375°F.

TO MAKE THE FILLING: Heat the oil in a large non-stick skillet over medium-high heat. Add the bell peppers, onion, jalapeño, and garlic; cook, stirring occasionally, until the bell peppers are tender, about 8 to 10 minutes. Remove the pan from the heat; stir in all the remaining filling ingredients. Taste and adjust the seasoning.

Place 2 tortillas on a baking sheet; sprinkle each with about 1/4 cup of the cheese. Leaving a 1-inch border, spread half of the bell pepper mixture on each tortilla. Sprinkle with the remaining cheese. Top each with another tortilla, pressing down gently to make the filling adhere.

Bake for about 8 minutes, or until the cheese is melted and the tortillas are softened and warm. Use kitchen shears or a pizza wheel (cutter) to cut each quesadilla into 6 wedges. Garnish with dollops of sour cream or add it to the plate on the side.

VARIATION

Rather than baking the assembled tortillas, toast them on a dry stovetop grill pan, preferably non-stick. Heat the pan over medium-high heat, then toast the quesadillas for about 4 to 6 minutes per side, or until the cheese is melted and grill marks are visible on the tortillas. (The result will be a char-grilled flavor and crispy-textured tortillas.)

Warm Veggie Hoagies

MAKES 2 SANDWICHES; SERVES 2

HEATING THESE SANDWICHES IN A MICROWAVE MAKES THE BUNS SOFT; FOR A CRUSTY TEXTURE, INDIVIDUALLY WRAP THE SANDWICHES IN FOIL AND HEAT THEM IN A PREHEATED 350°F OVEN FOR ABOUT 10 MINUTES, OR UNTIL THE CHEESE IS MELTED AND THE BREAD IS CRUSTY. TO SERVE A CROWD, MULTIPLY THIS RECIPE BY 4 AND SUBSTITUTE A LOAF OF ITALIAN BREAD FOR THE POOR BOY BUNS, THEN SLICE INTO SECTIONS FOR SERVING.

SPREAD
2 tablespoons Sun-Dried Tomato Pesto (page 15)

2 tablespoons mayonnaise

Pinch of red pepper flakes, or to taste

Two 6- to 8-inch poor boy (hoagie) buns, halved horizontally

VEGGIE FILLING
1 tomato, cut into 1/4-inch-thick slices

Dash of salt and freshly ground pepper to taste

Two 1/8-inch-thick slices red onion, separated into rings (optional)

1/2 cup thinly sliced mushrooms (see Tip)

1/4 green bell pepper, seeded, deveined, and cut into 1/4-inch-wide strips

1/2 cup (2 ounces) coarsely shredded mozzarella cheese

1/4 cup sliced ripe olives

1 cup finely shredded lettuce

ADVANCE PREPARATION
These sandwiches can be assembled up to 2 hours before serving; wrap them in plastic and refrigerate. Heat just before serving.

TO MAKE THE SPREAD: Stir all the ingredients together in a small bowl. Taste and adjust the seasoning.

Spread the cut sides of the buns with the spread. Top each bottom bun half with half of the filling ingredients in the order listed. Top each with an upper bun half, spread-side down. Fasten with long sandwich picks and cut in half diagonally.

TO HEAT: Place the sandwiches between 2 paper towels in a microwave. Heat on high for 1 minute, or until the buns are warmed and the vegetables are still crunchy. (Heating longer will make the buns soggy.)

VARIATION
Substitute slices of white or whole-wheat bread for the poor boy buns.

TIP

Refrigerate mushrooms for up to 4 days in a paper bag or in a basket so air can circulate around them. Before using, simply clean them with a mushroom brush or wipe with a moist paper towel. If necessary, rinse them quickly; mushrooms are very absorbent and should not be allowed to soak in water. Before using, cut off any woody stems and trim the bottoms off tender stems.

Tempeh Reubens

MAKES 4 SANDWICHES; SERVES 4

A VEGETARIAN SANDWICH BOOK WOULD BE INCOMPLETE WITHOUT THIS TWIST ON A CLASSIC DELI FAVORITE. SERVE ACCOMPANIED WITH ANOTHER UPDATED CLASSIC, LIKE SWEET POTATO AND ROMA TOMATO SALAD WITH WALNUT VINAIGRETTE (PAGE 118), MARINATED ANY-BEAN SALAD (PAGE 115), OR OVEN FRIES (PAGE 121).

TIPS

Dijon mustard, which originated in Dijon, France, is made from brown mustard seeds, spices, and white wine, making it more flavorful than ordinary yellow mustard.

Tempeh is made from cooked, fermented whole soybeans mixed with a grain such as brown rice, millet, or barley and formed into a cake. The flavor of tempeh is smoky and nutty; the texture is dense, chewy, and meaty. Tempeh is sold in natural foods stores and in some supermarkets, where it is found in the refrigerator or freezer section. It can be refrigerated in its package up to the stated expiration date; for longer storage, freeze tempeh for up to 6 months and thaw in the refrigerator before using.

8 slices dark rye bread

Honey Mustard (page 20) or Dijon mustard (see Tips) for spreading

FILLING

1 tablespoon olive oil

8 ounces tempeh, cut into four 1/4-inch-think pieces, 2 1/2 inches long by 2 inches wide (see Tips)

Four 1/8-inch-thick slices red onion, separated into rings

4 thin slices Swiss cheese (about 3 ounces)

1 cup canned or jarred sauerkraut, drained well

Four 3/8-inch-thick tomato slices

Spread one side of each slice of bread with mustard.

Heat the oil in a large nonstick skillet over medium-high heat. Add the tempeh and onion slices; turn the onion occasionally and cook the tempeh until lightly browned, about 4 to 5 minutes per side. Remove from the heat.

Layer each of 4 slices of bread with 1 slice of cheese, 1 piece of tempeh, one-fourth of the onions, 1/4 cup sauerkraut, and 1 tomato slice. Top each with a second bread slice, mustard-side down.

Coat a large nonstick skillet with cooking spray; heat over medium-high heat. Arrange the sandwiches in a single layer; heat until the cheese is melted and the bread is toasted, about 3 to 4 minutes per side. Cut the sandwiches in half diagonally and serve hot.

Vegetarian Sloppy Joes

MAKES 4 SANDWICHES; SERVES 4

NO ONE WILL MISS THE MEAT IN THIS VEGGIE VERSION OF AN OLD STANDBY. TEXTURIZED VEGETABLE PROTEIN (TVP) ASSUMES THE CONSISTENCY OF MEAT WHEN IT IS HYDRATED. ADD TOMATO SAUCE AND SEASONINGS AND THE COMBINATION IS MAGICAL. SERVE THESE BURGERS WITH MARINATED ANY-BEAN SALAD (PAGE 115).

FILLING

1 cup texturized vegetable protein (TVP); see Tip

¾ cup boiling water

1 tablespoon olive oil

½ cup coarsely chopped onion

½ cup coarsely chopped green or red bell pepper

4 cloves garlic, minced, or
2 teaspoons prepared minced garlic

One 8-ounce can tomato sauce

¼ cup water

2 tablespoons tomato paste

1 tablespoon packed light brown sugar

2 teaspoons Worcestershire sauce

2 teaspoons red wine vinegar

½ teaspoon freshly ground pepper, or to taste

¼ teaspoon salt, or to taste

4 whole-wheat hamburger buns, halved horizontally

Mayonnaise for spreading

ADVANCE PREPARATION
This filling will keep for up to 2 days in a covered container in the refrigerator. Reheat the filling, toast the buns, and assemble the sandwiches just before serving.

Preheat the oven to 375°F.

TO MAKE THE FILLING: Stir the texturized vegetable protein and boiling water together in a medium bowl; let stand until the water is absorbed and the TVP is softened, about 5 minutes.

Meanwhile, heat the oil in a large nonstick skillet over medium-high heat. Cook the onion, bell pepper, and garlic, stirring occasionally, until the bell pepper is tender, about 8 to 10 minutes.

Stir the remaining sandwich filling ingredients together in a medium bowl. Add this mixture and the softened TVP to the skillet; stir until the mixture is bubbly. Reduce the heat to low and cook, stirring occasionally, for about 5 minutes. Taste and adjust the seasoning.

Arrange the buns, cut sides up, on a baking sheet. Toast in the oven for about 4 minutes, or until the cut surfaces are lightly browned. Lightly spread each with mayonnaise. Spoon one fourth of the filling over the mayonnaise on the bottom half of each bun; top with the upper half.

TIP

Texturized vegetable protein (TVP) is a dry, granulated product made from compressed soy flour. It is found in natural foods stores and in some supermarkets. Store TVP in an airtight container at room temperature for up to 2 months. Before using, TVP must be hydrated by combining it with boiling water; when moistened, it doubles in volume.

Italian Toasted Cheese Sandwiches

MAKES 2 SANDWICHES; SERVES 2

TOASTED CHEESE SANDWICHES, A TIME-HONORED TRADITION IN ITALY, ARE MADE WITH *PANE IN CASSETTA*, THE SAME BREAD USED FOR TRAMEZZINI. SOLD ALONGSIDE BASIC TRAMEZZINI IN ITALIAN WINE BARS, THEY ARE TOASTED USING A HINGED GRILL THAT LIGHTLY BROWNS BOTH SIDES OF THE SANDWICH AT THE SAME TIME. YOU CAN ACHIEVE THE EFFECT AT HOME BY USING A STOVETOP GRILL PAN (SEE TIPS). TRY CREATING SOME OF YOUR OWN VARIATIONS.

TIPS

Stovetop grill pans are available in a variety of materials (including nonstick, which I recommend), and they come in a range of shapes, sizes, and prices. What they have in common is raised ridges on the cooking surface that give foods cooked on the pan visually appealing grill lines, along with a smoky, grilled flavor achieved quickly indoors with little or no added fat.

To make your own spray oil, pour oil into a small container fitted with a pump sprayer. (Use a travel spray container from a drugstore or a specially designed oil-spray can from a gourmet shop.) Use to oil baking and cooking pans in place of commercially-produced nonstick cooking sprays. This also is a way to apply a light touch of oil to green salads.

4 slices white sandwich bread, crusts removed

Herb Butter (page 22) for spreading

Four 1/8-inch-thick slices (about 3 ounces) Havarti cheese, or other mild-flavored cheese

1/2 Roasted Red Bell Pepper (page 26) or jarred roasted red bell pepper, well drained, cut into 1/2-inch-wide strips

Lightly spread one side of each bread slice with the herb butter.

Top each of 2 slices of bread with 2 slices of cheese and half of the bell pepper strips. Top each with a second slice of bread, buttered-side down.

Heat a stovetop grill pan (see Tips) over high heat. (If the pan does not have a nonstick surface, lightly coat it with olive oil; see Tips.) Reduce the heat to medium-high. Place the sandwiches on the grill and toast, pressing down occasionally with a spatula, until the cheese is melted and the bread is lightly browned, with visible grill marks, about 1 1/2 minutes on each side. Cut the sandwiches in half and serve hot.

VARIATIONS

Substitute Swiss cheese for the Havarti cheese and thin tomato slices for the bell pepper strips.

Substitute Brie cheese for the Havarti cheese and thin slices of peeled pear for the bell pepper strips; garnish with fresh watercress.

Savory Nut Patties on Sesame Buns

MAKES 4 BURGERS; SERVES 4

HERE'S MY ALTERNATIVE TO HAMBURGERS. ORDINARY KETCHUP IS THE CONDIMENT OF CHOICE, WITH A JUICY DILL ON THE SIDE AND A GENEROUS HELPING OF OVEN FRIES (PAGE 121) OR HAZELNUT–GREEN BEAN SALAD (PAGE 113).

---

4 sesame hamburger buns, halved horizontally

Mayonnaise or Garlic Mayonnaise (page 21) and/or mustard for spreading

SAVORY NUT PATTIES

1 cup finely chopped walnuts (about 4 ounces), preferably toasted (see Tips)

1/4 cup cottage cheese

1/4 cup dried bread crumbs

1 egg, lightly beaten

1 tablespoon soy sauce

1 tablespoon finely chopped onion

1 tablespoon minced fresh flat-leaf parsley

2 cloves garlic, minced, or 1 teaspoon prepared minced garlic

1 teaspoon minced fresh thyme, or 1/4 teaspoon dried thyme

1 tablespoon olive oil

4 lettuce leaves or 4 cups alfalfa sprouts (see Tip, page 71)

Four 1/4-inch-thick tomato slices

Eight 1/4-inch-thick avocado slices (optional)

ADVANCE PREPARATION
The patty mixture will keep for up to 2 days in a covered container in the refrigerator. Cook the patties and assemble the sandwiches just before serving.

Preheat the oven to 375°F. Arrange the buns, cut-sides up, on a baking sheet. Toast in the oven for about 4 minutes, or until the cut surfaces are lightly browned. Spread them with mayonnaise and/or mustard.

TO MAKE THE PATTIES: Combine all the patty ingredients except the oil in a medium bowl. Form the mixture into 4 patties about 3 1/2 inches in diameter and 1/2 inch thick. Heat the oil in a large nonstick skillet over medium-high heat. Cook the patties until lightly browned, about 3 minutes on each side.

Layer the bottom half of each bun with lettuce or sprouts, a patty, a tomato slice, and 2 avocado slices. Top with the upper half of the bun.

VARIATION

Spread the cut sides of the buns with Guacamole (page 18); when assembling the sandwiches, omit the avocado slices and mayonnaise.

TIPS

Because of their high fat content, nuts quickly become rancid at room temperature. Shelled nuts can be refrigerated in an airtight container for up to 4 months or frozen for up to 6 months. To freshen their flavor, spread the nuts on a baking sheet and heat in a preheated 150°F oven for a few minutes.

TOASTING NUTS: Toasting enhances the flavor and texture of most nuts. To toast nuts on the stovetop, put them in a dry skillet over medium-high heat. Stir or toss, watching closely, until they are golden brown, about 4 to 5 minutes. If you prefer, nuts can be toasted on a baking sheet or pie plate in a preheated 375°F oven for 5 to 10 minutes, stirring frequently. To prevent burning, remove the nuts from the skillet or baking pan as soon as they are toasted.

Portobello Mushroom Burgers

MAKES 4 BURGERS; SERVES 4

THESE ARE GOURMET BURGERS FOR ADULTS, SO USE CRUSTY BUNS IF YOU PREFER. ADD A SPEARED KALAMATA OLIVE, AND ACCOMPANY THE BURGERS WITH POTATO SALAD WITH LEMON VINAIGRETTE (PAGE 117) OR SWEET POTATO AND ROMA TOMATO SALAD WITH WALNUT VINAIGRETTE (PAGE 118).

------

4 whole-wheat hamburger buns, halved horizontally

**Garlic Mayonnaise (page 21),
Basil Mayonnaise (page 21),
Marinated Goat Cheese (page 23),
or Honey Mustard (page 20) for spreading**

Preheat the oven to 375°F. Arrange the buns, cut-sides up, on a baking sheet. Toast in the oven for about 4 minutes, or until the cut surfaces of the buns are lightly browned. Spread them with your choice of mayonnaise, cheese, or mustard.

BURGERS

2 tablespoons olive oil

1/4 cup minced onion

**4 cloves garlic, minced, or
2 teaspoons prepared minced garlic (see Tips)**

**3 cups diced portobello mushroom caps
(about 3 large mushroom caps)**

1/2 cup finely shredded carrot

**1/2 cup packaged garlic and herb-seasoned
dried bread crumbs**

1 egg, lightly beaten

1/8 teaspoon freshly ground pepper, or to taste

TO MAKE THE BURGERS: Heat 1 tablespoon of the oil in a large nonstick skillet over medium-high heat. Add the onion and garlic; cook, stirring constantly, until aromatic and tender, about 2 minutes. Add the mushrooms and carrot; continue to cook until tender, about 4 more minutes.

Transfer the mixture to a bowl and let cool. Stir in the remaining burger ingredients except the oil. Form the mixture into 4 burgers about 3 1/2 inches in diameter and 1/2 inch thick. Heat the remaining 1 tablespoon oil in a large nonstick skillet over medium-high heat. Cook the patties until lightly browned, about 4 minutes per side.

4 tender lettuce leaves, such as red leaf lettuce

Four 1/4-inch-thick tomato slices

Layer the bottom half of each bun with lettuce, a burger, and a tomato slice. Top with the upper half of the bun and serve hot.

Open-Faced Breakfast Sandwiches

MAKES 2 SANDWICHES; SERVES 2

THE AROMA OF WARM CINNAMON ROLLS IS ALWAYS ENTICING. I LEARNED TO MAKE THIS SIMPLE VERSION WHEN I WAS A CHILD, AND IT HAS BEEN A FAVORITE SUNDAY MORNING BREAKFAST SANDWICH EVER SINCE. SERVE A HEAPING SPOONFUL OF APRICOT, PEAR, AND APPLE CHUTNEY (PAGE 28) ON THE SIDE OR GARNISH THE PLATE WITH A STRAWBERRY FAN (SEE TIP, PAGE 127).

2 whole-grain English muffins, split horizontally

2 tablespoons butter at room temperature

1 tablespoon packed light brown sugar (see Tip)

¼ teaspoon ground cinnamon

2 tablespoons sliced almonds

Preheat the broiler. Place the English muffins on a baking sheet. Broil 4 to 5 inches from the heat source for about 2 minutes per side, or until lightly toasted. Or, toast in a toaster.

Combine the butter, brown sugar, and cinnamon in a small bowl. Spread half of the butter mixture on the cut side of each of 2 English muffin halves; sprinkle each with half of the almonds. Broil for about 2 minutes, or until the spread is bubbly and the almonds are lightly browned. Serve hot.

TIP

Brown sugar is made of white sugar combined with molasses, which gives it a soft texture. It is available in both light and dark varieties; the lighter the color, the milder the flavor. Hardened brown sugar can be softened by placing an apple wedge in the jar or bag of sugar; seal tightly for 1 or 2 days.

Croissants Stuffed with Herbed Scrambled Eggs, Spinach, Apples, and Brie

MAKES 2 SANDWICHES; SERVES 2

SERVE THESE HEARTY SANDWICHES AS A SPECIAL TREAT FOR BRUNCH OR LUNCH. GARNISH THE PLATES WITH SMALL BUNCHES OF JUICY RED GRAPES TO ADD COLOR AND CRUNCH, AND ACCOMPANY WITH TALL GLASSES OF FRESHLY SQUEEZED ORANGE JUICE.

----

8 stemmed spinach leaves

2 large croissants, halved horizontally

FILLING
1/2 large apple, cored, peeled, and quartered

4 eggs

2 tablespoons milk

1 tablespoon butter

2 ounces Brie cheese
cut into 1/2 -inch chunks (1/3 cup); see Tips

2 tablespoons snipped fresh chives

Freshly grated nutmeg to taste (see Tips)

Salt and freshly ground pepper to taste

Arrange 4 spinach leaves on the bottom half of each croissant.

TO MAKE THE FILLING: Cut each apple quarter crosswise into 1/4-inch-thick slices. Beat the eggs lightly with a fork in a small bowl, then add the milk and beat lightly again; set aside. Melt the butter in a medium nonstick skillet over medium heat. Add the apple slices; cook, stirring occasionally, until the slices are nearly tender, about 3 minutes. Reduce the heat to medium-low; add the egg mixture. As it begins to set, use a spatula to move the cooked portion to the side, allowing the uncooked portion to spread over the bottom. (This will take about 1 minute.)

While the egg mixture is still very moist, reduce the heat to low; dot with the Brie and sprinkle with the chives, nutmeg, salt, and pepper. Fold some of the cooked egg mixture over the Brie so it will melt. Remove the pan from the heat before the egg mixture becomes either dry or browned on the edges. Taste and adjust the seasoning.

Spoon half of the cooked egg mixture over the spinach on each croissant half. Top with the other half of the croissant. Serve hot, with forks.

Omelet Focaccia Sandwiches

MAKES 6 SANDWICHES; SERVES 6

HERBES DE PROVENCE IS ONE OF MY FAVORITE SEASONINGS FOR EGGS, BUT YOU CAN SUBSTITUTE ABOUT 1 TABLESPOON MINCED FRESH HERBS, SUCH AS BASIL, OREGANO, OR A COMBINATION.

One 8-inch round or square onion focaccia or plain focaccia, halved horizontally

Butter, Herb Butter (page 22), fresh white goat cheese, or Marinated Goat Cheese (page 23) for spreading; at room temperature

FILLING
4 eggs

2 tablespoons cold water

1 teaspoon herbes de Provence (see Tip)

1 tablespoon olive oil

1 cup thin onion slices

2 cloves garlic, minced, or 1 teaspoon prepared minced garlic

2 tablespoons butter

1 1/2 cups coarsely shredded stemmed spinach leaves

1/2 cup (2 ounces) coarsely shredded Romano cheese

1 Roasted Red Bell Pepper (page 26) or jarred roasted red bell pepper, well drained, cut into 1/2-inch-wide strips

Salt and freshly ground pepper to taste

Preheat the oven to 300°F. Spread the cut sides of the focaccia with the butter or cheese.

TO MAKE THE FILLING: Whisk the eggs and water, just until blended, in a medium bowl, then whisk in the herbes de Provence; set aside. Heat the oil in a medium nonstick skillet over medium-high heat. Add the onion slices; cook, stirring constantly, until they are translucent, about 4 minutes. Add the garlic and cook for 1 more minute. Transfer the mixture to a bowl and cover.

Melt the butter in the same skillet over medium-high heat; pour in the egg mixture. Cook undisturbed for about 30 seconds, then as the edges become firm, push them toward the center, so the uncooked portions can reach the hot pan surface. Tilt the pan and move the cooked portions as necessary until the egg is still moist but no longer runny, about 3 minutes. Slide the omelet, without folding it, from the skillet onto the bottom half of the focaccia.

Layer the remaining filling ingredients on the top of the omelet in this order: the cooked onion mixture, spinach, cheese, and bell pepper strips. Sprinkle with salt and pepper. Top with the upper half of the focaccia.

Wrap the sandwich in aluminum foil. Place it on a baking sheet and bake for about 15 minutes, or until the bread is heated through and the cheese is melted. Use a serrated knife to slice the focaccia into 6 wedges or squares and serve hot.

TIP

Herbes de Provence is a mixture of dried herbs commonly containing basil, fennel seeds, lavender, marjoram, rosemary, sage, summer savory, and thyme. It is most often imported from the South of France, where it is a traditional flavoring. The herb blend can be found in small clay crocks in gourmet shops and some supermarkets.

Stuffed pita bread and tortilla wraps enlarge the world of sandwich possibilities. Tabbouleh and hummus in pitas is a vegetarian tradition. Salads can become meals on the go when they are stuffed into pita bread pockets. Asian Roasted Vegetable Wraps (page 109) and Mexican Black Bean Pitas (page 104) fuse different cuisines. Create some of your own combinations using spreads and fillings throughout this book. The sandwich knows no borders, so explore possibilities and have fun.

Keep these guidelines in mind: Make your wraps with white flour tortillas rather than corn, which in my opinion are better in baked and sauced dishes. Thanks to their newfound popularity, flour tortillas are now available in many flavors, such as garlic, jalapeño, and basil. And you'll find them in many colors, such as tomato red and spinach green. Freshly made tortillas are best, but for convenience you can purchase good-quality tortillas in supermarket packages. I usually select tortillas labeled "home style," because they are slightly thicker and do not split once the sandwich is made.

Pita bread is available also in several varieties. First of all, make certain that you are purchasing Mediterranean or Greek pocket bread rather than flat, Lebanese pita bread, which has no pocket for stuffing. Pita pockets are available made with either white-flour or whole-wheat flour, and some even contain other ingredients, such as oat bran, or other grains and flavorings, such as garlic and onion. I usually buy white flour pitas because they are more moist. When buying pitas, check the expiration date; pita breads dry out quickly. For that reason, I rarely freeze pitas; after freezing, it may be necessary to moisten them with a little water, wrap them in aluminum foil, and heat them briefly in a preheated 350°F oven. Some brands are thicker than others. Thicker pitas have a better texture, and the edges stay intact while you are eating, keeping the filling in the sandwich. To make a pita sandwich, open one end for a single deep pocket or cut the pita in half vertically to form 2 half-round smaller sandwiches.

Ratatouille in Pitas

MAKES 8 SANDWICHES; SERVES 4

LEFTOVER RATATOUILLE IS GREAT TO HAVE ON HAND TO USE AS A FILLING FOR OMELETS OR CRÊPES, AS A TOPPING FOR BAKED POTATOES, OR AS AN ENTRÉE ACCOMPANIMENT.

RATATOUILLE

2 tablespoons olive oil

1 cup 3/8-inch-wide onion strips (see Tips)

1 eggplant (about 1 pound), peeled and cut into 2-by-3/8-inch strips (about 4 cups)

1 zucchini, cut into 2-by-3/8-inch strips (about 2 cups)

8 ounces green beans, cut into 2-inch-long pieces (about 2 cups)

1/2 green bell pepper, seeded, deveined, and cut into 2-by-3/8-inch strips

4 cloves garlic, minced, or 2 teaspoons prepared minced garlic

3 tablespoons red wine vinegar

One 15-ounce can chunky tomato sauce

1 teaspoon sugar

1 tablespoon minced fresh basil, or 1/2 teaspoon dried basil

2 teaspoons minced fresh oregano, or 1/2 teaspoon dried oregano

1/2 teaspoon freshly ground pepper, or to taste

1/4 teaspoon salt, or to taste

2 large tomatoes

Four 7-inch pita bread rounds, each cut to form 2 half-rounds

Finely shredded lettuce and finely shredded Cheddar or Monterey jack cheese for garnish

TO MAKE THE RATATOUILLE: Heat the oil in a Dutch oven or large pot over medium-high heat. Add the onion; cook, stirring occasionally, until it is glossy, about 3 minutes. Reduce the heat to medium-low. Stir in the eggplant, zucchini, green beans, bell pepper, and garlic. Drizzle the vinegar over the vegetables. Cover and cook, stirring occasionally, for about 10 minutes. (Reduce the heat if the vegetables start to brown.)

Reduce the heat to low. Add the tomato sauce, sugar, dried basil and oregano (if using), pepper, and salt. Cover and cook, stirring occasionally, until the green beans are tender, about 30 minutes.

Meanwhile, peel the tomatoes (see Tip, page 101), then cut into 1/2-inch cubes.

Remove the pan from the heat. Stir in the tomatoes and fresh basil and oregano (if using). Cover and let stand for about 30 minutes. Taste and adjust the seasoning.

Split open each pita half and fill it with about 3/4 cup ratatouille. Garnish with lettuce and cheese.

ADVANCE PREPARATION
The ratatouille will keep for up to 4 days in a covered container in the refrigerator. Bring to room temperature or reheat. Assemble the sandwiches just before serving.

TIPS

Onions will keep for up to 2 months if stored in a cool, dry, and dark place with good air circulation. If you prefer, refrigerate them for up to 1 week; because of the humidity, longer refrigeration will cause spoilage. Chop leftover onion, store it in a refrigerator container or a self-sealing plastic bag, and use within 4 days or freeze for up to 2 months.

Tear-producing vapors can be reduced by refrigerating an onion for several hours or freezing it for 20 minutes before chopping.

After cooking, yellow, or Spanish, onions usually have a sweeter flavor than white onions. Another rule of thumb is that the flatter the onion, the sweeter it is. Red, or Italian, onions are also mild and often are used raw.

Middle Eastern
Pita Pockets

MAKES 8 SANDWICHES; SERVES 4

THE TWO MIDDLE EASTERN CLASSICS, HUMMUS (PAGE 17) AND TABBOULEH, COMPLEMENT EACH OTHER.
BOTH ARE BEST IF MADE A DAY IN ADVANCE, MAKING THIS COOL, REFRESHING SANDWICH A
QUICK-TO-ASSEMBLE, LIGHT MEAL AT THE END OF A FUN-FILLED HOT SUMMER DAY.

TIP

The staple grain of the Middle East is bulgur wheat, or cracked wheat. In processing, the wheat is steamed and dried, then cracked into small, granular pieces. It is sold in natural foods stores and supermarkets, where it is usually stocked with either the rice or hot cereals. Bulgur, which has a unique nutty flavor, is available in coarse, medium, or fine fragments; select the smallest fragments for use in tabbouleh. Store it in an airtight container in a cool, dry place.

TABBOULEH

1 1/2 cups vegetable stock

3/4 cup fine-grain bulgur wheat (see Tip)

1/4 cup fresh lemon juice

2 tablespoons extra-virgin olive oil

2 tablespoons coarsely chopped fresh mint

1/4 teaspoon freshly ground pepper, or to taste

1/8 teaspoon ground cinnamon, or to taste

1/8 teaspoon salt, or to taste

Ground allspice to taste

Freshly grated nutmeg to taste

1 tomato, cut into 1/2-inch cubes

1/2 cup finely chopped celery

1/2 cup finely chopped cucumber

1/3 cup finely chopped green onions, including green tops

1/4 cup minced fresh flat-leaf parsley

Four 7-inch multi-grain pita bread rounds, each cut to form 2 half-rounds

1 cup Hummus (page 17)

8 romaine lettuce leaves

ADVANCE PREPARATION
In separate covered containers in the refrigerator, the hummus will keep for up to 5 days, and the tabbouleh will keep for up to 3 days.

TO MAKE THE TABBOULEH: Bring the vegetable stock to a boil in a small covered saucepan. Remove the pan from the heat. Stir in the bulgur wheat; cover and set aside until the liquid is completely absorbed and the bulgur is softened, about 30 to 40 minutes.

While the bulgur is soaking, whisk together the lemon juice and olive oil. Stir in the mint, pepper, cinnamon, salt, allspice, and nutmeg.

Transfer the bulgur wheat to a large bowl; add all the remaining tabbouleh ingredients and toss. Whisk the lemon juice mixture, add it to the bulgur wheat, and toss again. Taste and adjust the seasoning. Refrigerate in a covered container for at least 1 hour before serving.

Split open each pita half and spread the inside with 2 tablespoons hummus. Insert a romaine leaf and fill with 1/2 cup tabbouleh.

Marinated Fresh Mozzarella, Tomato, and Basil Salad in Pitas

MAKES 4 SANDWICHES; SERVES 2

MAKE THESE SANDWICHES IN THE SUMMER WHEN TOMATOES ARE AT THEIR JUICY BEST AND FRESH BASIL IS PLENTIFUL. BE SURE TO SELECT FRESH MOZZARELLA AT AN ITALIAN MARKET, A CHEESE SHOP, OR IN THE SPECIALTY CHEESE SECTION OF THE SUPERMARKET. THIS SOFT WHITE CHEESE HAS A DELICATE TEXTURE AND MILD FLAVOR, AND IS VERY DIFFERENT FROM THE TYPE OF MOZZARELLA OFTEN USED ON PIZZA.

MARINADE

2 tablespoons red wine vinegar

2 tablespoons extra-virgin olive oil

1 tablespoon minced fresh basil

1 clove garlic, minced, or
½ teaspoon prepared minced garlic

½ teaspoon grated lemon rind (see Tip, page 28)

¼ teaspoon freshly ground pepper, or to taste

Salt to taste

1 large tomato, peeled (see Tip) and
cut into ½-inch cubes

3 ounces fresh mozzarella cheese,
cut into ½-inch cubes (½ cup)

Two 7-inch pita bread rounds, each
cut to form 2 half-rounds

4 leaves red leaf lettuce

ADVANCE PREPARATION
The tomato and cheese will keep in the marinade for up to 2 days in a covered container in the refrigerator. Assemble the sandwiches just before serving.

TO MAKE THE MARINADE: Whisk all the ingredients together in a small bowl.

Combine the tomato and cheese cubes in a shallow dish. Drizzle with the marinade. Cover and refrigerate for about 1 hour. Taste and adjust the seasoning.

Split the pita halves open and line each with a lettuce leaf. Use a slotted spoon to add the tomato mixture to the pita halves.

TIP

PEELING TOMATOES: To peel a tomato, first core it with a paring knife, removing the stem end and white center. Cut an X on the bottom of the tomato, carefully piercing through just the skin. Immerse the tomato in a pot of boiling water just long enough to loosen the skin without cooking the tomato (5 seconds for a very ripe tomato, 10 to 20 seconds for a firmer tomato). Remove the tomato with a slotted spoon and immediately plunge it into a bowl of very cold water; let stand for about 1 minute. When the tomato is cool enough to handle, use a paring knife to slip off the skin.

Greek Tomato and Feta Salad Sandwiches

MAKES 8 SANDWICHES; SERVES 4

My love of this salad prompted me to find a creative way to serve it. Tucked into a fresh, moist pita, the salad is ideal for a light summer lunch. It needs no accompaniment. Assemble these sandwiches just before serving, because the dressing quickly softens the bread.

FILLING

4 cups coarsely shredded stemmed spinach leaves or romaine lettuce

2 Roma (plum) tomatoes, halved lengthwise, each half cut into 1/8-inch-thick slices

1/2 cucumber, halved lengthwise, each half cut into 1/8-inch-thick slices (about 1 cup)

1/2 cup (2 ounces) crumbled feta cheese (see Tip)

1/4 cup coarsely chopped onion

1/4 cup sliced pitted kalamata olives

2 tablespoons coarsely chopped fresh basil leaves

1/2 cup Lemon Vinaigrette (page 24)

Four 7-inch plain pita bread rounds, each cut to form 2 half-rounds

Freshly ground pepper to taste

TO MAKE THE FILLING: Toss all the filling ingredients except the vinaigrette in a medium bowl. Whisk the vinaigrette, add it to the bowl, and toss again. Taste and adjust the seasoning.

Split open and stuff each pita half with about 1/2 cup of the salad mixture; sprinkle with pepper.

TIP

Feta cheese is a white Greek cheese with a tangy flavor. Traditionally, it is made with goat's milk, sheep's milk, or a combination; today, it is also often made with cow's milk. Fresh feta is crumbly; when mature, it becomes drier and saltier.

Mexican Black Bean Pitas

MAKES 8 SANDWICHES; SERVES 4

IN MY HOME, WE HAVE DIFFERING OPINIONS ON CILANTRO. I OMIT IT FOR MY SON, BUT ADD A HEALTHY DOSE OF MINCED FRESH CILANTRO TO MY PORTION OF THIS FILLING. WE AGREE THAT IT'S NECESSARY TO HAVE A SPICY PEPPERONCINI ON THE SIDE. USE YOUR FAVORITE BOTTLED SALSA FOR THIS RECIPE: HOT, MEDIUM, OR MILD TO SUIT YOUR PREFERENCE. GARNISH THE PLATES WITH SLICED ORANGES, AND FOR AN ACCOMPANIMENT, CUT LEFTOVER JICAMA INTO STRIPS, TOSS THEM IN FRESH LIME JUICE, AND DIP THE ENDS INTO CHILI POWDER.

TIPS

Jicama, sometime called the Mexican potato, is a large, bulbous root vegetable. Beneath its thin brown skin is a white water chestnut–textured flesh with a sweet flavor. Store it sealed in a plastic bag for up to 2 weeks in the refrigerator. Peel before using.

Black beans, also called turtle beans, are a member of the kidney bean family. Black on the outside, cream colored within, they keep their shape and sweet, hearty flavor after cooking. Canned black beans are available in most supermarkets. Do not confuse them with the Asian black bean, which is a type of soybean that is fermented with salt and used as a flavoring.

Cumin, an essential ingredient in chili powder and curry powder, is the dried fruit of a plant in the parsley family. Available in both whole seed and ground forms, it provides an aromatic nutty and peppery flavor, and is widely used in Mexican and Indian cooking. Store it in a cool, dark place, where it will keep for up to 6 months.

FILLING

1 large tomato, cut into ½-inch cubes

1 green bell pepper, seeded, deveined, and coarsely chopped

1 cup jicama in 1-by-¼-inch strips (see Tips)

¼ cup coarsely chopped red onion

One 15-ounce can black beans, drained and rinsed (see Tips)

1 tablespoon fresh lime juice

½ cup bottled salsa

¼ teaspoon ground cumin (see Tips)

Salt and freshly ground pepper to taste

Four 7-inch onion-flavored or plain pita bread rounds, each cut to form 2 half-rounds

⅔ cup Guacamole (page 18)

Shredded Cheddar cheese and/or sour cream for garnish

ADVANCE PREPARATION
This filling will keep for up to 3 days in a covered container in the refrigerator. Assemble the sandwiches just before serving.

TO MAKE THE FILLING: Toss the tomato, bell pepper, jicama, onion, and beans together in a medium bowl. Add all the remaining filling ingredients and toss again. Taste and adjust the seasoning.

Split open each pita half and spread the inside with a heaping tablespoon of guacamole. Use a slotted spoon to add about ½ cup of the filling into each pita. Top with your choice of garnish.

VARIATION
Spread the pitas with mustard or Honey Mustard (page 20); omit the guacamole.

Mediterranean Roll-Ups with Feta-Kalamata Spread

MAKES 2 SANDWICHES; SERVES 2

To speed preparation, use packaged shredded broccoli-coleslaw mix, which usually contains colorful julienned carrots and shredded red cabbage, available in supermarket produce departments. The vegetables are left raw and crunchy, making this a refreshing choice for a hot summer day. It's fine to use plain floured tortillas, but try using colorful tomato-flavored tortillas when they are available. You can prepare the roll-ups in advance to serve as a light lunch or as an appetizer for carefree entertaining.

FETA-KALAMATA SPREAD
1/4 cup cream cheese at room temperature

1/4 cup crumbled feta cheese

4 kalamata olives, finely chopped (see Tip)

1 tablespoon extra-virgin olive oil

1 tablespoon red wine vinegar

1 teaspoon minced fresh oregano

1 clove garlic, minced, or
1/2 teaspoon prepared minced garlic

Two 7-inch flour tortillas

1 1/2 cups broccoli-coleslaw mix

1 Roma (plum) tomato,
cut into 1/8-inch-thick slices

Freshly ground pepper to taste

TO MAKE THE SPREAD: Combine all the ingredients in a small bowl; stir until blended.

Spread each tortilla to the edges with half of the feta mixture. Top with half of the coleslaw mix and a horizontal row of half of the tomato slices. Sprinkle with pepper. Roll up firmly; wrap in plastic wrap and refrigerate for at least 15 minutes.

Unwrap the roll and trim to even the ends. For sandwiches, slice each roll-up diagonally into 3 sections. For appetizer servings, slice each roll-up into 6 sections.

VARIATION
Substitute Marinated Goat Cheese (page 23) for the Feta-Kalamata Spread.

ADVANCE PREPARATION
This spread will keep for up to 2 days in a covered container in the refrigerator. The plastic-wrapped roll-ups can be refrigerated for up to 4 hours before serving.

TIP

Kalamata olives are eggplant-colored, almond-shaped Greek olives, ranging in length from about 1/2 to 1 inch. The rich and fruity-flavored olives are packed in olive oil, brine, or wine vinegar, and they are often slit to allow the marinade in which they are soaking to be absorbed into the flesh.

Italian Roasted Vegetable Wraps

MAKES 2 SANDWICHES; SERVES 2

TO VARY THE VEGETABLES IN THIS RECIPE, TRY ROASTED PORTOBELLO MUSHROOM CAPS AND RED BELL PEPPER STRIPS. TO MAKE THE WRAPS A BIT MORE FILLING, STIR SOME COOKED CANNELLINI BEANS INTO THE ROASTED VEGETABLES.

MARINADE

3 tablespoons fresh lemon juice

2 tablespoons balsamic vinegar

2 tablespoons extra-virgin olive oil

1 tablespoon soy sauce

2 cloves garlic, minced, or
1 teaspoon prepared minced garlic

2 teaspoons minced fresh rosemary

Four 1/4-inch-thick crosswise slices peeled eggplant

1 small zucchini,
cut into 1/4-inch-thick slices

1/2 small yellow summer squash,
cut into 1/4-inch-thick slices

1 cup thinly sliced fennel (about 1 bulb); see Tips

Two 10-inch flour tortillas

2 tablespoons Basil Mayonnaise (page 21)

4 fresh arugula leaves

Dash of freshly ground pepper

2 tablespoons freshly grated Parmesan cheese

TO MAKE THE MARINADE: Whisk all the ingredients together in a shallow bowl.

Add the vegetables to the marinade and toss. Cover or transfer to a self-sealing plastic bag and refrigerate for at least 1 hour or for up to 8 hours.

Preheat the broiler. Use a slotted spoon to transfer the vegetables to a lightly oiled jelly roll pan; discard the remaining marinade. Broil the vegetables 4 to 5 inches from the heat source, stirring occasionally, for about 10 to 12 minutes, or until they are tender and lightly browned. Cut the eggplant slices into 1/4-inch-wide strips. Set the vegetables aside to cool.

Warm the tortillas (see Tips). Spread 1 tablespoon of the mayonnaise horizontally across the bottom half of each tortilla, so that it is about 1 inch from the sides. Top each tortilla with 2 arugula leaves and half of the vegetables; sprinkle with pepper and half of the Parmesan cheese. Fold the right and left sides of a tortilla inward toward the center and over the filling; next, fold the bottom edge upward toward the center and then firmly roll the wrap away from you until it completely wraps the filling. Repeat with the second tortilla. Serve immediately at room temperature. Or, if you prefer, heat the wraps. Wrap in aluminum foil and heat in a preheated 350°F oven for about 10 minutes. Or, wrap in paper towels and heat in the microwave on high for about 2 minutes. Leave the wraps whole to contain the juicy contents.

Asian Roasted Vegetable Wraps

MAKES 2 SANDWICHES; SERVES 2

THE KEY TO TASTY ROASTED VEGETABLES IS THE MARINATING MIXTURE.

MARINADE
¼ cup soy sauce

¼ cup white rice vinegar

2 tablespoons canola oil

2 tablespoons mirin (see Tips) or dry sherry

1 clove garlic, minced, or
½ teaspoon prepared minced garlic

Dash of ground white pepper

1 small yellow summer squash,
cut into 2-by-¼-inch strips

2 large white mushrooms,
cut into ¼-inch-thick slices

½ red bell pepper, seeded, deveined, and
cut into 2-by-½-inch strips

¼ red onion, cut into ¼-inch-thick slices

Two 10-inch flour tortillas

2 tablespoons Apricot-Orange Sauce (page 29),
bottled Chinese plum sauce (see Tips), or
bottled hoisin sauce (see Tips)

½ cup cooked rice,
preferably basmati or jasmine

TO MAKE THE MARINADE: Whisk all the ingredients together in a shallow bowl.

Add the vegetables to the marinade and toss. Cover bowl or transfer to a self-sealing plastic bag and refrigerate for at least 1 hour or for up to 8 hours.

Preheat the broiler. Use a slotted spoon to transfer the vegetables to a lightly oiled jelly roll pan; discard the remaining marinade. Broil the vegetables 4 to 5 inches from the heat source, stirring occasionally, for about 10 to 12 minutes, or until they are tender and lightly browned. Set aside to cool.

Warm the tortillas (see Tip, page 108). Spread 1 tablespoon of the sauce horizontally across the bottom half of each tortilla, so that the sauce is about 1 inch from the sides. Top with ¼ cup of the rice and half of the vegetables. Fold the right and left sides of a tortilla inward toward the center and over the filling; next, fold the bottom edge upward toward the center and then firmly roll the tortilla away from you until it completely wraps the filling. Repeat with the second tortilla. Serve immediately. Or, if you prefer, heat the wraps: Wrap in aluminum foil and heat in a preheated 350°F oven for about 10 minutes. Or, wrap in paper towels and heat in the microwave on high for about 2 minutes. Leave the wraps whole to contain the juicy contents.

VARIATION
In addition to the roasted vegetables, add fresh mango strips when filling the wraps.

sandwich
ACCOMPANIMENTS

Accompaniments can be as simple as carrot and celery sticks or sliced fruit. Others will turn your sandwiches into complete and filling meals. Many can be purchased in cans, jars, and bags on supermarket shelves, but nothing beats the aroma of home-made soup on the stove. Deli potato salad drenched in mayonnaise just doesn't compare to my Potato Salad with Lemon Vinaigrette (page 117) made with the best extra-virgin olive oil and freshly squeezed lemon juice.

Think in terms of color, texture, temperature, and ethnic theme when you pair accompaniments with your sandwiches. When you're serving a sandwich on dark rye bread, add color to the plate with Sweet Potato and Roma Tomato Salad with Walnut Vinaigrette (page 118). Use a crispy accompaniment, like Apple-Cranberry Salad (page 116), with a grilled sandwich oozing with creamy cheese. If you're serving Dilled Egg Salad Sandwiches with Vegetables (page 67) on a chilly day, add warmth with Herbed Fresh Tomato-Carrot Soup (page 120) on the side. Carry out the Mexican theme by accompanying your Black Bean Quesadillas (page 80) with Red Pepper and Green Apple Relish with Cilantro Vinaigrette (page 119).

Hazelnut–Green Bean Salad

MAKES 4 SERVINGS

HAZELNUT OIL LENDS ITS DISTINCTIVE FLAVOR AND AROMA TO THIS SALAD. SERVE THE MIXTURE ATOP SPICY ARUGULA LEAVES ALONGSIDE GRILLED PORTOBELLO MUSHROOM SANDWICHES WITH SUN-DRIED TOMATO AND GOAT CHEESE SPREAD (PAGE 73) FOR A MEMORABLE MEAL.

(PAGE 73)

HAZELNUT VINAIGRETTE
1/4 cup hazelnut oil (see Tip)

3 tablespoons red wine vinegar

2 tablespoons extra-virgin olive oil

1 teaspoon Dijon mustard

1/8 teaspoon freshly ground pepper, or to taste

1/8 teaspoon salt, or to taste

12 ounces green beans cut into 2-inch lengths (about 3 cups)

1/2 cup minced red bell pepper

2 tablespoons minced onion

ADVANCE PREPARATION
This salad will keep for up to 3 days in a tightly closed container in the refrigerator.

TO MAKE THE VINAIGRETTE: Whisk the vinaigrette ingredients together in a small bowl; set aside.

Steam the beans over boiling water in a covered pot for about 5 minutes, or until crisp-tender. Or, put the green beans in a medium microwave-proof dish; add about 1/4 cup water. Cover tightly and microwave on high for about 5 minutes (depending on the thickness of the beans). Rinse with cold water and drain well.

Transfer the beans to a medium bowl. Add the bell pepper and onion; toss. Whisk the vinaigrette; add it to the salad and toss again. Taste and adjust the seasoning. Use a slotted spoon to serve the beans.

TIP
Hazelnut oil, most often imported from France, is fragrant and full-flavored, tasting like the roasted nut. Because of its strong flavor, this oil is usually used in combination with a lighter oil. To prevent rancidity, store hazelnut oil in the refrigerator, where it will keep for up to 3 months.

Marinated
Oven-Dried Tomatoes

MAKES 6 SERVINGS

OVEN-DRYING IS ANOTHER WAY TO ENJOY TOMATOES WHEN THEY ARE AT THEIR SUMMER BEST AND IN GENEROUS SUPPLY. THE TOMATOES BECOME SWEETER AFTER DRYING, AND MARINATING ADDS AN EXTRA BURST OF FLAVOR. FOR SHORTER PREPARATION TIME, BAKE THE TOMATOES FOR JUST 2 TO 3 HOURS, UNTIL THEY ARE JUST PARTIALLY SHRIVELED, THEN TOSS THEM WITH SOME FRESH TOMATO HALVES AND SERVE THE MIXTURE ATOP MIXED BABY GREENS FOR A CONTRAST IN TEXTURE AND FLAVOR.

TIPS

Freshly ground or cracked whole dried peppercorns are more flavorful than preground pepper because the peppercorn immediately releases oil as aroma and flavor when it is cracked. The best pepper grinders have settings for both coarse and fine grinds. To measure, grind the pepper onto a sheet of waxed paper and pour into a measuring spoon. For coarser chunks of pepper, crack whole peppercorns by crushing on a cutting board with the side of a French chef's knife. Store whole peppercorns in a cool, dark place for up to 1 year.

SEEDING TOMATOES: Cut the tomato in half and, holding each half in the palm of your hand, gently squeeze out the seeds.

¼ cup extra-virgin olive oil

4 cloves garlic, minced, or
2 teaspoons prepared minced garlic

2 teaspoons cracked black pepper (see Tips)

½ teaspoon salt

2 pounds ripe Roma (plum) tomatoes
(about 8 to 12 tomatoes), halved
lengthwise and seeded (see Tips)

ITALIAN MARINADE
¼ cup extra-virgin olive oil

¼ cup white wine vinegar

1 tablespoon minced shallot

1 teaspoon minced fresh flat-leaf parsley

1 teaspoon minced fresh oregano, or
¼ teaspoon dried oregano

⅛ teaspoon dry mustard

Pinch of red pepper flakes, or to taste

Dash of ground white pepper, or to taste

Fresh basil or oregano sprigs for garnish

ADVANCE PREPARATION
The marinated oven-dried tomatoes will keep for up to 1 week in a covered container in the refrigerator. Bring to room temperature for serving.

Preheat the oven to 175°F. Cover a large baking sheet with aluminum foil. Stir the olive oil, garlic, pepper, and salt together in a medium bowl. Add the tomatoes to the olive oil mixture and toss. Use a slotted spoon to transfer the tomatoes, cut-sides up, onto the baking sheet. Bake in the oven for 6 to 8 hours or overnight. The tomatoes should be shriveled, but still retain some moisture and softness.

TO MAKE THE MARINADE: While the tomatoes are in the oven, whisk all the marinade ingredients together in a medium bowl. Refrigerate in a covered container.

When the tomatoes are done, whisk the marinade. Add the tomatoes and toss. (If you prefer, first halve the tomatoes again lengthwise or cut them into smaller pieces.) Taste and adjust the seasoning. Use a slotted spoon to serve the tomatoes. Garnish with fresh basil or oregano sprigs.

VARIATIONS
Substitute Lemon Vinaigrette (page 24) or Balsamic Marinade (page 115) for the Italian Marinade.

Marinated Any-Bean Salad

MAKES 6 SERVINGS

USE ANY COMBINATION OF YOUR FAVORITE BEANS IN THIS HEARTY SALAD. PLAN AHEAD TO ALLOW AT LEAST A FEW HOURS BEFORE SERVING, BECAUSE THE BEANS WILL ABSORB THE MARINADE AND THE DELECTABLE FLAVORS WILL BLEND.

BALSAMIC MARINADE

3 tablespoons balsamic vinegar (see Tip)

3 tablespoons extra-virgin olive oil

2 tablespoons fresh lemon juice

1 tablespoon minced fresh basil, or 1/2 teaspoon dried basil

4 cloves garlic, minced, or 2 teaspoons prepared minced garlic

1 teaspoon Dijon mustard

1 teaspoon packed light brown sugar

1/4 teaspoon freshly ground pepper, or to taste

1/8 teaspoon salt, or to taste

1/2 cup thinly sliced red onion

Two 15-ounce cans beans (black beans, garbanzo beans, kidney beans, or a combination), drained and rinsed

1/2 cup diced green bell pepper

1/4 cup diced red bell pepper

2 tablespoons coarsely chopped fresh flat-leaf parsley

ADVANCE PREPARATION
This salad will keep for up to 4 days in a tightly closed container in the refrigerator.

TO MAKE THE MARINADE: Whisk all the ingredients together in a small bowl.

Cover the onion with ice water in a medium bowl. Let stand for about 20 minutes; drain and pat dry.

Toss the onion and all the remaining ingredients together in the bowl. Whisk the marinade; add it to the salad and toss again. Taste and adjust the seasoning. Use a slotted spoon to serve the beans.

TIP

Balsamic vinegar (the Italian *aceto balsamico*) is a wine vinegar made by boiling the juice of white Trebbiano grapes in copper pots until it caramelizes. The vinegar is then aged for up to thirty years in barrels made from various woods (oak, chestnut, mulberry, and juniper), each adding a hint of its woody flavor. The result is a vinegar with a heavy, mellow, almost-sweet flavor, and a dark color. Store balsamic vinegar in a cool, dark place for up to 6 months after opening.

Apple-Cranberry Salad

MAKES 4 SERVINGS

TART CRISPY RED AND GREEN APPLES AND SWEET-TART DRIED CRANBERRIES IN A CREAMY DRESSING OF
PURE MAPLE SYRUP CREATE A SALAD OF NOTABLE FLAVORS, TEXTURES, AND COLORS. APPLES AND WALNUTS ARE
SPLENDID COMPLEMENTS TO CHEESE SANDWICHES.

TIP

Paprika is a powder made from ground sweet red pepper pods. Most paprika comes from Spain, South America, California, or Hungary; the Hungarian is considered by many to be the best. Hungarian paprika comes in 3 levels of hotness: mild (often labeled "sweet"), hot, and exceptionally hot. To preserve its color and flavor, store paprika in a cool, dark place for no longer than 6 months.

CREAMY MAPLE DRESSING

1/4 cup sour cream

2 tablespoons pure maple syrup

1 tablespoon fresh lemon juice

1 tablespoon mayonnaise

1/4 teaspoon celery seeds

1/4 teaspoon dry mustard

Dash of sweet paprika, preferably Hungarian (see Tip)

Dash of salt, or to taste

1 large unpeeled red apple, cored and cut into 1/2-inch cubes

1 large unpeeled green apple, cored and cut into 1/2-inch cubes

1/4 cup coarsely chopped toasted walnuts (see Tip, page 89)

1/4 cup dried cranberries

ADVANCE PREPARATION
This dressing will keep for up to 2 days in a tightly closed container in the refrigerator. Toss the salad up to 2 hours before serving.

TO MAKE THE DRESSING: Whisk all the ingredients together in a small bowl.

Toss all the remaining ingredients together in a medium bowl. Add the dressing and toss again. Taste and adjust the seasoning.

VARIATION
Substitute pears, preferably 1 green and 1 crimson, for the apples; substitute pecans for the walnuts.

Potato Salad with Lemon Vinaigrette

MAKES 6 SERVINGS

UNLIKE TYPICAL AMERICAN POTATO SALAD, THIS ONE CONTAINS NO MAYONNAISE. TO ADD COLOR TO THE PLATE,
SERVE A MOUND OF THE SALAD ATOP A THIN TOMATO SLICE.

---

1 1/2 pounds unpeeled new red potatoes, scrubbed (see Tip)

1 large tomato, cut into 1/4-inch-thick slices

1/2 cup coarsely chopped green onions, including green tops

1/4 cup coarsely chopped celery leaves

1/2 cup Lemon Vinaigrette (page 24)

ADVANCE PREPARATION
This salad will keep for up to 2 days in a tightly closed container in the refrigerator. Bring to room temperature for serving.

Cook the potatoes in salted boiling water until just tender, about 15 to 18 minutes. Drain and rinse with cool water, then drain again. Let cool to the touch.

Cut the potatoes into quarters; transfer them to a medium bowl. Add the tomato, green onions, and celery leaves in a medium bowl; toss gently. Whisk the dressing; add it to the salad and toss again. Use a slotted spoon to serve the salad.

TIP

New red potatoes are young potatoes that are harvested before maturity. They are small, thin-skinned, low in starch, and sweet in flavor. They cook rapidly when boiled or steamed. New potatoes are not recommended for baking or mashing, but they are preferable for potato salads, because mature baking potatoes break apart too easily and absorb too much of the dressing. Store new potatoes for up to 2 weeks at room temperature in a cool, dark place. Do not store potatoes in the refrigerator, because the cold will convert their starch to sugar, causing them to become sweet and to darken when cooked.

Sweet Potato and Roma Tomato Salad with Walnut Vinaigrette

MAKES 4 SERVINGS

SERVE THIS DO-AHEAD SALAD WITH PORTOBELLO MUSHROOM BURGERS (PAGE 90) OR GRILLED PORTOBELLO MUSHROOM SANDWICHES WITH SUN-DRIED TOMATO AND GOAT CHEESE SPREAD (PAGE 73) FOR A GOURMET APPROACH TO SANDWICH DINING.

TIP

Walnuts are 60 percent oil. The oil has a pleasant, nutty taste and is used mainly for salads rather than as a cooking medium. For the best flavor and aroma, select a high-quality brand made from roasted walnuts. Read the labels; inexpensive nut oils are likely to be a blend containing only a small percent of nut oil. Like other nut oils, walnut oil quickly turns rancid at room temperature; it will keep for up to 3 months in the refrigerator.

WALNUT VINAIGRETTE

1/4 cup red wine vinegar

3 tablespoons roasted walnut oil (see Tip)

1 teaspoon Dijon mustard

1/2 teaspoon sugar

1/8 teaspoon freshly ground pepper, or to taste

Salt to taste

1 tablespoon minced fresh flat-leaf parsley

1 large orange-fleshed sweet potato (about 14 ounces), peeled and cut into 2-inch-thick slices

2 Roma (plum) tomatoes, cut into 1/2-inch cubes

1 green onion (including green tops), coarsely chopped

Chopped toasted walnuts (see Tip, page 89) for garnish

ADVANCE PREPARATION
This salad will keep for up to 3 days in a tightly closed container in the refrigerator. Bring to room temperature before serving.

TO MAKE THE VINAIGRETTE: Whisk all the ingredients, except the parsley, together in a small bowl; add the parsley.

Cook the sweet potato in salted boiling water until fork-tender, about 15 minutes. Or, steam the potato over boiling water in a covered pot for about 8 to 10 minutes. Drain and rinse with cold water, then drain again. Cut the potato into 1-inch chunks.

Toss the potato, tomatoes, and green onion in a medium bowl. Whisk the vinaigrette; add it to the salad and toss again. Taste and adjust the seasoning. Use a slotted spoon to serve the salad. Garnish each serving with walnuts.

Red Pepper and Green Apple Relish with Cilantro Vinaigrette

MAKES 6 SERVINGS

THE CRISP, TART FLAVORS AND VIBRANT COLORS OF THIS RELISH MAKE IT AN AMIABLE COMPANION FOR ROASTED RED PEPPER–AVOCADO CLUBS WITH WHITE BEAN HUMMUS (PAGE 64) OR MEXICAN BLACK BEAN PITAS (PAGE 104).

CILANTRO VINAIGRETTE

3 tablespoons canola oil

2 tablespoons red wine vinegar

1 tablespoon fresh lemon juice

1/2 jalapeño chile, seeded and minced (about 1/2 tablespoon), or to taste (see Tip, page 80)

1/2 teaspoon Honey Mustard (page 20) or horseradish mustard

1/2 teaspoon sugar

1/8 teaspoon ground cumin

1/8 teaspoon freshly ground pepper, or to taste

Salt to taste

1 tablespoon minced fresh cilantro (see Tips)

1/2 red bell pepper, seeded, deveined, and cut into 2-by-1/16-inch strips

1/2 tart green apple, peeled, cored and cut into julienne

1/2 cup slivered red onion

ADVANCE PREPARATION
This relish will keep for up to 2 days in a covered container in the refrigerator.

TO MAKE THE VINAIGRETTE: Whisk all the ingredients, except the cilantro, together in a small bowl; add the cilantro.

Toss all the remaining ingredients together in a medium bowl. Whisk the vinaigrette; add it to the relish and toss again. Taste and adjust the seasoning.

TIPS

Cilantro, also called fresh coriander or Chinese parsley, is commonly used for its distinctive pungent flavor and fragrance in Vietnamese, Thai, other Asian, Indian, and Mexican cuisines. Choose leaves with a bright, even color and no sign of wilting. The dried leaves lack fresh cilantro's distinctive flavor and are an unacceptable substitution.

Ground coriander, an ingredient in most curry powders, is made from the ground seeds of the plant and serves a different purpose from that of coriander leaves.

Herbed Fresh Tomato-Carrot Soup

MAKES 6 CUPS; SERVES 4 TO 6

AS A CHILD, I LOVED COMING HOME TO THE AROMA OF TOMATO SOUP HEATING ON THE STOVE. I THOUGHT IT WAS UMM-UMM GOOD WITH A SIMPLE CHEESE SANDWICH. TIME DOESN'T ALTER THOSE SIMPLE PLEASURES. HERE'S A QUICK-TO-PREPARE, GROWN-UP TOMATO SOUP TO PAIR WITH SOPHISTICATED SANDWICHES. SERVE IT CHILLED ON WARM SUMMER DAYS.

TIPS

When stored in a tightly closed tin or glass container (rather than in a box) in a dark, dry place, dried herbs will remain flavorful for about 1 year; it's a good idea to date the jars when you buy them. They should resemble the color they were when fresh and should not be dull or brownish-green. To get the most flavor out of your dried herbs, crumble them between your fingers to release the aromatics as you add them to your recipes.

Fresh herbs, which come from the leafy part of plants, contain more moisture and therefore are milder than dried herbs. When substituting, use 3 to 4 times more fresh herbs than dried herbs.

PURÉEING SOUPS: Although a food processor has become the appliance of choice for many culinary tasks, a smooth consistency for puréed soups and sauces is best achieved by using a blender.

2 tablespoons olive oil

1 cup finely chopped carrots (about 2 carrots)

¼ cup finely chopped celery

¼ cup minced shallots

2 ½ pounds tomatoes, peeled (see Tip, page 101) and cut into 1-inch cubes (about 5 cups)

3 cups tomato juice

2 tablespoons minced fresh basil, or 1 teaspoon dried basil (see Tips)

1 teaspoon minced fresh thyme, or ¼ teaspoon dried thyme (see Tips)

1 teaspoon sugar

1 bay leaf

½ teaspoon freshly ground pepper, or to taste

Salt to taste

Dollops of fresh white goat cheese or freshly grated Parmesan cheese for garnish

ADVANCE PREPARATION
This soup will keep for up to 3 days in a covered container in the refrigerator. Reheat or serve chilled.

Heat the oil in a Dutch oven over medium heat. Add the carrots and celery; cook, stirring occasionally, for about 4 minutes. Add the shallots; continue to cook, stirring constantly, until the vegetables are tender, about 1 more minute.

Stir in the tomatoes, tomato juice, dried basil and thyme (if using dried herbs), sugar, bay leaf, pepper, and salt. Stir occasionally until the mixture comes to a boil; cover and cook for about 10 minutes. Remove the bay leaf.

In 2 batches, transfer the mixture to a blender and blend until smooth. (If you prefer a chunky soup, blend only half of the soup mixture.)

Stir in the fresh basil and thyme (if using fresh herbs). Taste and adjust the seasoning. Reheat the soup, if necessary.

Serve piping hot, each serving topped with goat cheese or Parmesan cheese. Or refrigerate and serve later, chilled.

Oven Fries

MAKES 2 SERVINGS

FOR SOME, SANDWICHES ARE INCOMPLETE WITHOUT A SIDE OF FRIES. THE GOOD NEWS IS THAT THEY CAN BE MADE BY OVEN ROASTING, WITHOUT THE MESS OR CALORIES OF DEEP-FAT FRYING. HERE'S A SIMPLE METHOD FOR PREPARING GARLICKY FRIES IN THE OVEN.

---

1 large unpeeled baking potato, scrubbed and cut into 3-by-$\frac{3}{8}$-inch strips

1 tablespoon garlic-infused olive oil

Salt to taste

Preheat the oven to 450°F. Soak the potato strips in cold water for about 10 minutes. Drain well and roll in a clean dish towel to dry. Toss the strips with the olive oil in a medium bowl.

Spread the strips in a single layer on a baking sheet (see Tip). Bake, turning occasionally, for about 25 minutes, or until the strips are lightly browned and crispy.

Press the baked strips between sheets of paper towels. Discard the towels and transfer the fries to a serving bowl. Sprinkle with salt. Serve hot.

TIP

When buying baking sheets, select stainless steel instead of aluminum. Aluminum sheets will bend and buckle when heated, resulting in an uneven surface.

DESSERT sandwiches

What's cool and tempting on hot and humid summer days? Ice cream sandwiches, of course! Making them is child's play: matching favorite cookies with the best ice cream. Better yet, start by making homemade cookies.

Chocolate-Filled Baked French Toast Sandwiches (page 127) team layers of egg-soaked bread and dark chocolate into an ambrosial finale to a light dinner or for a decadent late-night snack.

Chocolate Chip Ice Cream Sandwiches

MAKES 10 SANDWICHES; SERVES 10

BAKE THE COOKIES ON A COOL SUMMER DAY AND ASSEMBLE THEM TO FREEZE FOR THE STEAMY DAYS AHEAD.
IF TIME IS LIMITED, BUY THIN CHOCOLATE WAFERS OR USE YOUR FAVORITE COOKIES FROM THE BAKERY.

WHOLE-WHEAT CHOCOLATE CHIP–OATMEAL COOKIES

¾ cup whole-wheat flour

¼ cup toasted wheat germ (see Tip)

½ teaspoon baking soda

¼ teaspoon ground cinnamon

¼ teaspoon salt

½ cup (1 stick) unsalted butter at room temperature

½ cup granulated sugar

½ cup packed light brown sugar

1 egg

2 teaspoons pure vanilla extract

1 cup old-fashioned rolled oats

1 cup semisweet chocolate chips

2 pints vanilla, chocolate, or strawberry ice cream, or another flavor of your choice

ADVANCE PREPARATION

Ice cream sandwiches will keep for up to 2 weeks in the freezer; put the single-wrapped sandwiches in a freezer bag or freezer container or double-wrap them in plastic. The texture of the cookies softens after being frozen.

Preheat the oven to 375°F. Spray 2 baking sheets with nonstick cooking spray. Position 2 oven racks in the center and upper third of the oven.

TO MAKE THE COOKIES: Stir the flour, wheat germ, baking soda, cinnamon, and salt together in a medium bowl. Put the butter and sugars in another medium bowl; use an electric mixer on medium speed to beat until creamy, about 1 minute. Add the egg and vanilla; beat on low speed until well combined, about 15 seconds. Gradually add the flour mixture and beat until thoroughly combined. Stir in the oats and chocolate chips.

Use a small (2 tablespoon) ice cream scoop to make twenty 1½-inch balls of the dough; place them about 2 inches apart on the baking sheets. Press down the tops of the balls just slightly. Bake for 12 to 14 minutes, rotating the baking sheets halfway through the baking time for even browning; the cookies should be lightly browned and still slightly soft in the center. Place each baking sheet on a wire rack for about 3 minutes, then use a spatula to transfer the cookies to wire racks to cool.

Let the ice cream soften slightly. (You can put it in the refrigerator for about 5 minutes.) Spoon ice cream into a ½-cup measuring cup. Turn it out onto the flat bottom of a cookie. Top with a second cookie, flat side down. Press gently. Repeat with the remaining cookies. Wrap in plastic and freeze until firm, at least 1 hour.

TIP

Wheat germ, the embryo of the wheat berry, is rich in vitamins, minerals, and protein. Toasted wheat germ, found in the cereal aisle of most supermarkets, is preferable to raw wheat germ in most recipes because of its nutty flavor and slightly crunchy texture. To prevent rancidity, store toasted wheat germ for up to 6 months in a tightly closed container in the refrigerator.

Chocolate-Filled Baked French Toast Sandwiches

MAKES 6 SANDWICHES; SERVES 6

MY FRIEND FRAN LEBAHN SHARED THIS BAKED SANDWICH RECIPE WITH ME; IT GARNERS RAVE REVIEWS IN HER CHOCOLATE CLASSES. IT'S A BIT TOO SUBSTANTIAL FOR DESSERT AFTER A FULL MEAL, BUT JUST RIGHT FOR A HEARTY SNACK. TRY THE JAM VARIATION FOR BRUNCH.

Six 4-inch-diameter, 1-inch-thick diagonal slices French bread

4 ounces semisweet chocolate, broken into large chunks

3 eggs

1 cup milk

3 tablespoons granulated sugar

1 teaspoon pure vanilla extract

1/2 teaspoon ground cinnamon

1/4 teaspoon salt

2 tablespoons unsalted butter

Confectioners' sugar and 6 strawberries or strawberry fans (see Tip) for garnish

ADVANCE PREPARATION
The assembled sandwiches must be refrigerated for at least 2 hours or overnight; bake just before serving.

Cut horizontally through each slice of bread with a serrated knife to within 1/4 inch of the bottom crust, forming a pocket. Stuff each pocket with chocolate chunks, then press the slices closed. Arrange the filled slices in an 8-by-8-inch buttered baking dish.

Whisk the eggs lightly in a medium bowl, then whisk in the milk, sugar, vanilla, cinnamon, and salt. Pour over the bread; let it soak in for about 10 minutes. Turn the sandwiches over. Cover the dish with plastic wrap and refrigerate for at least 2 hours. The egg mixture will be totally absorbed.

Preheat the oven to 425°F. Remove the dish from the refrigerator for about 15 minutes before baking. Melt the butter; pour it over the sandwiches. Bake for 25 to 30 minutes, or until the sandwiches are golden brown and set.

Transfer the warm sandwiches to individual plates. Dust them with confectioners' sugar stirred through a fine strainer; garnish each with a strawberry or strawberry fan and serve immediately with forks.

VARIATION
Cut the bread into twelve 1/2-inch-thick diagonal slices. Spread 6 of the slices with about 2 teaspoons of jam (I like strawberry, raspberry, or apricot); top with the remaining bread slices. For the 1 cup milk, substitute 3/4 cup milk plus 1/4 cup fruit liqueur, such as Grand Marnier or Triple Sec.

TIP
MAKING A STRAWBERRY FAN: Choose a firm, red strawberry. Place it, hull down, on a cutting board and make parallel cuts in the berry from the pointed end nearly to the leaves; take care not to slice all the way through. (The number of cuts will depend on the size of the berry.) Hold the strawberry gently and twist so that the slices fan out. The hull can be left intact or removed and replaced with a small sprig of fresh mint.